A GUIDE TO
IRELAND'S
MOUNTAIN SUMMITS
THE VANDELEUR-LYNAMS
& THE ARDERINS

with additional information and data derived from
the collective efforts of the contributors to the
Mountainviews.ie website

The Collins Press

First published in 2013 by
The Collins Press
West Link Park
Doughcloyne
Wilton
Cork

© text and maps MountainViews.ie 2013

British Library Cataloguing in Publication Data
A guide to Ireland's mountain summits : the
Vandeleur-Lynams & the Arderins.
1. Mountaineering—Ireland–Guidebooks. 2. Ireland–
Guidebooks.
I. MountainViews.
796.5'22'09415-dc23

ISBN-13: 9781848891647

Design & typesetting by Brendan O'Reilly

Typeset in Myriad Pro

Printed in Poland by Białostockie Zakłady Graficzne SA

All text and photos in this book have been created
by members of MountainViews

CONTENTS

ACKNOWLEDGEMENTS

The committee of the MountainViews community are pleased to acknowledge the following contributions to the creation of this book, apologising to anyone we missed.

Original list data: from Michael Dewey, Myrddyn Phillips, and Joss Lynam as detailed in the Appendix.

Name research: Paul Tempan for extensive research in Irish and English. See http://mountainviews.ie/features/names/revisednames2/MVlist2008.htm

List correction: John FitzGerald, Mark Brennan, Colin Dalton, Brendan O'Reilly, Paul Tempan, John Desmond and Paul Donnelly. John FitzGerald for determining heights to around 10cm, so far for over 50 summits.

Crowd sourced data: To the 48 MountainViews members, so far, who submitted 1,966 GPS readings for summits, and the 1,241 members who submitted 7,913 summit ratings.

Book creation: Simon Stewart and Colin Murphy for articles. Eleven photographers (see p. 123). Brendan O'Reilly for putting this book together with regard to design, layout and typesetting, and The Collins Press.

Framework: Simon Stewart who designed and created the means for recording and sharing data and for the global open-source community for making tools available including Linux, MySQL, PHP, OpenLayers & jQuery. Map sources from OSM and Ordnance Survey Ireland.

All contributions have been made without financial payment in any form. Any profits to be administered by the committee to the benefit of MountainViews and the glorious sport of hillwalking.

Simon Stewart, Founder of MountainViews.ie

MOUNTAINVIEWS HILL AREAS: NORTH

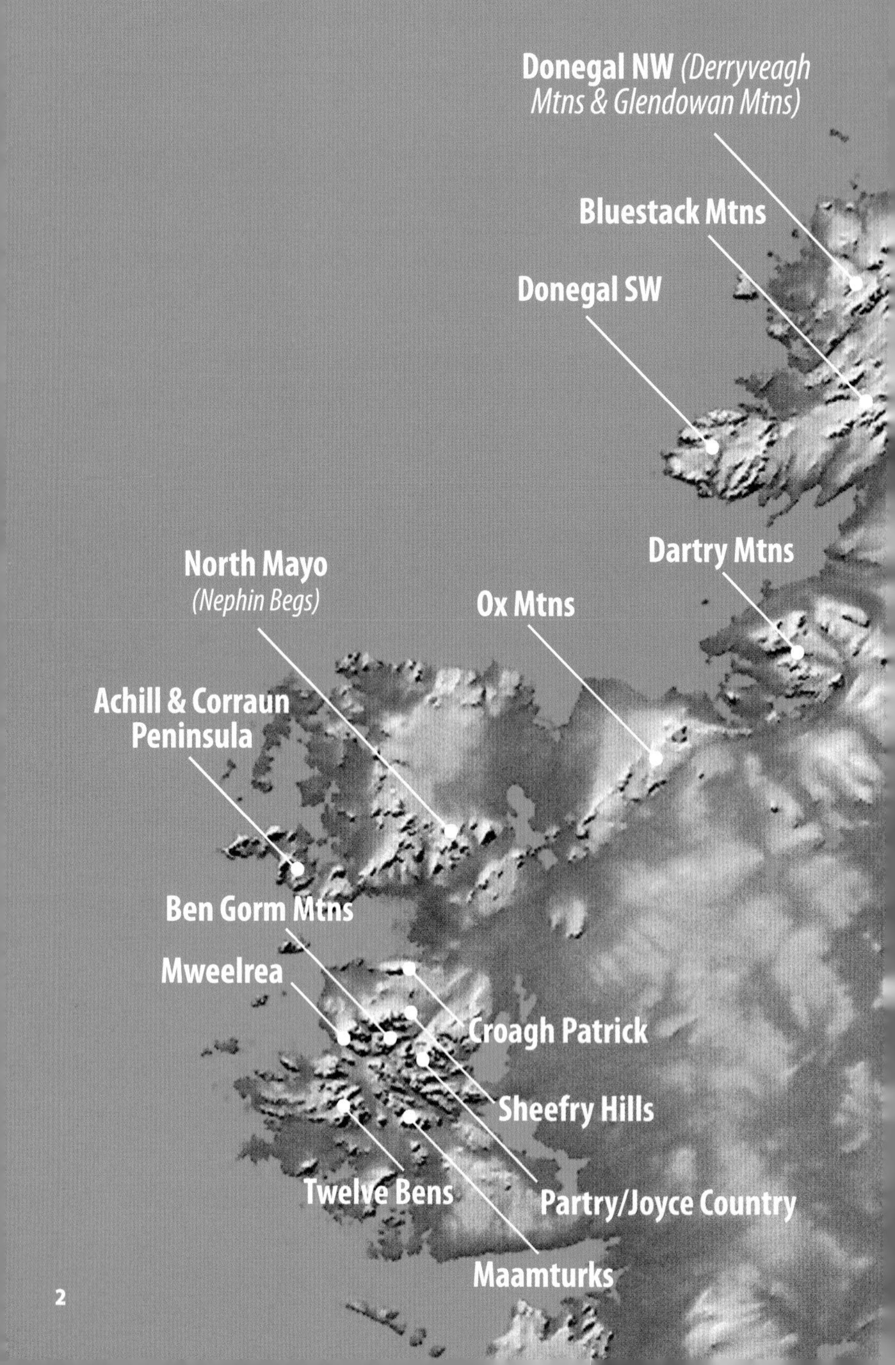

Donegal NW *(Derryveagh Mtns & Glendowan Mtns)*
Bluestack Mtns
Donegal SW
Dartry Mtns
North Mayo
(Nephin Begs)
Ox Mtns
Achill & Corraun Peninsula
Ben Gorm Mtns
Mweelrea
Croagh Patrick
Sheefry Hills
Twelve Bens
Partry/Joyce Country
Maamturks

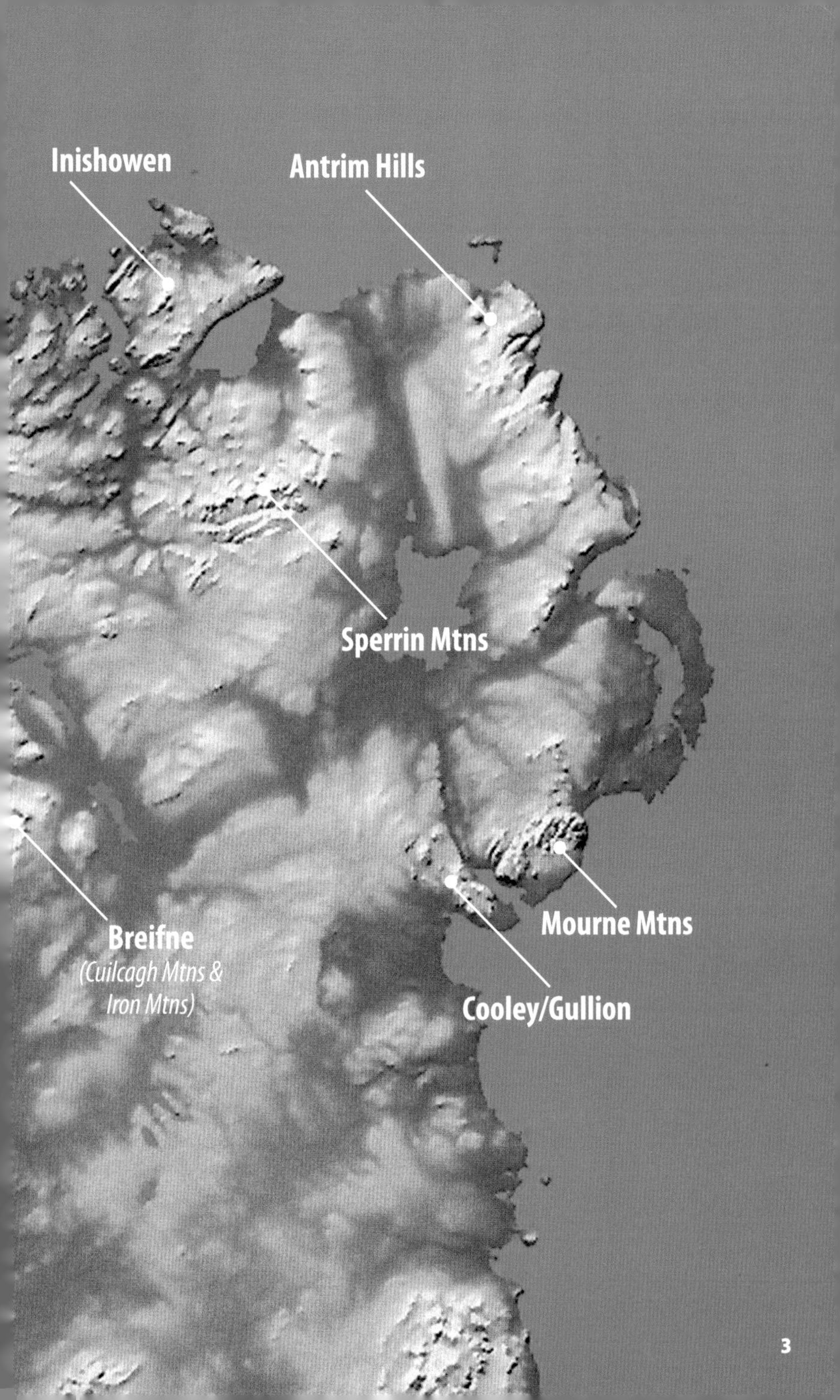

Inishowen

Antrim Hills

Sperrin Mtns

Mourne Mtns

Breifne
(Cuilcagh Mtns &
Iron Mtns)

Cooley/Gullion

3

MOUNTAINVIEWS HILL AREAS: SOUTH

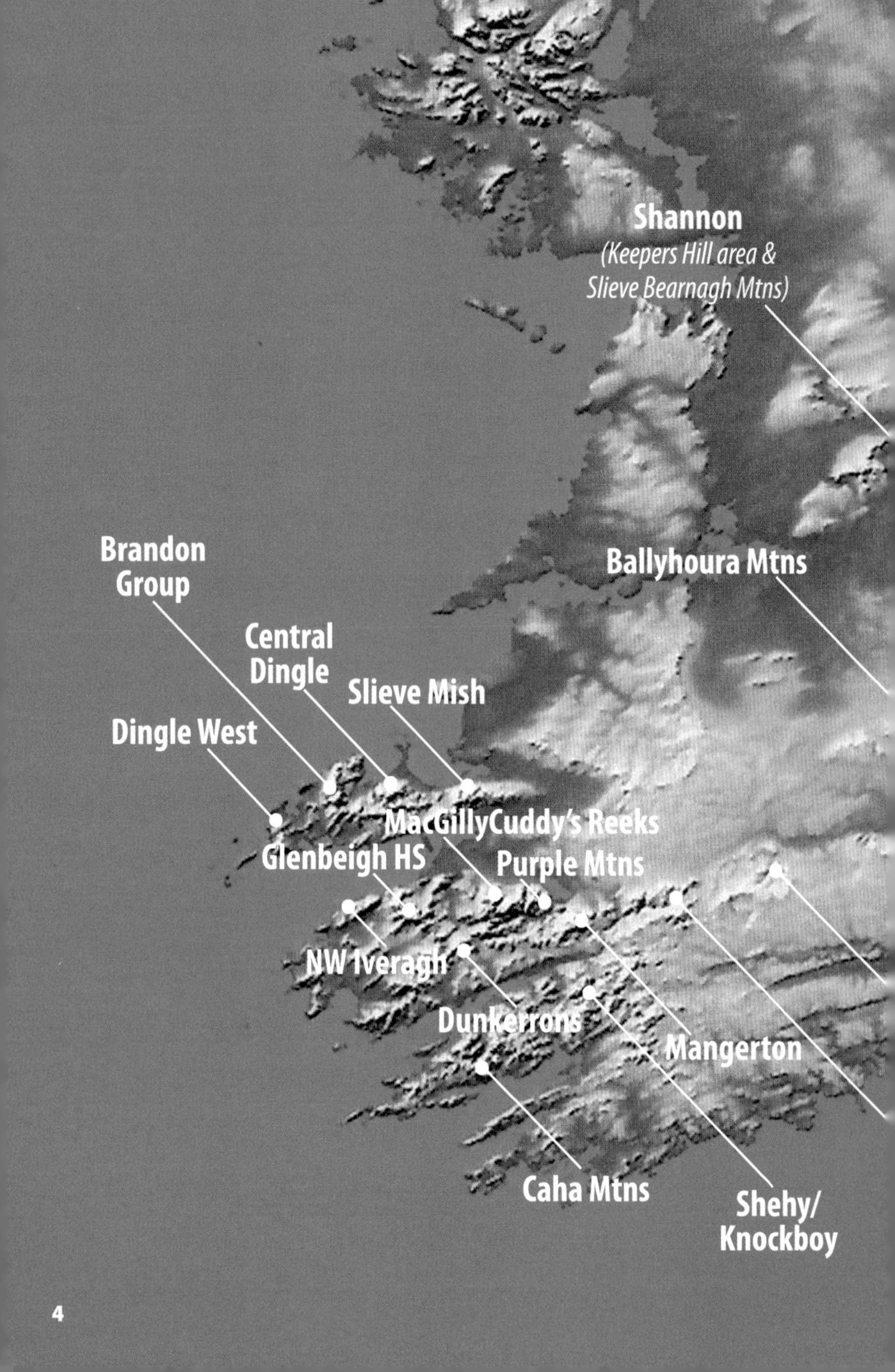
Shannon
(Keepers Hill area &
Slieve Bearnagh Mtns)
Brandon
Group
Central
Dingle
Slieve Mish
Ballyhoura Mtns
Dingle West
MacGillyCuddy's Reeks
Glenbeigh HS
Purple Mtns
NW Iveragh
Dunkerrons
Mangerton
Caha Mtns
Shehy/
Knockboy

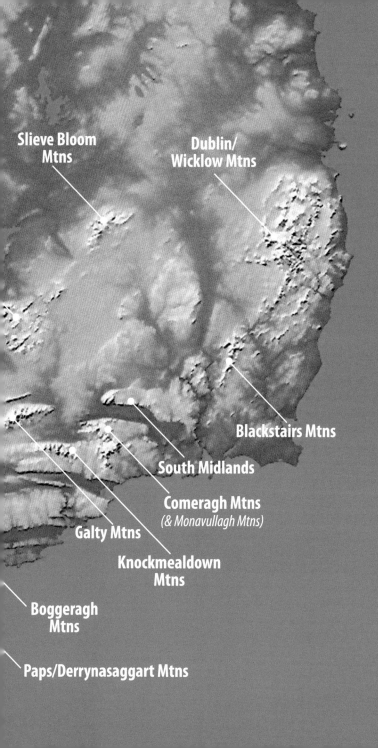

Slieve Bloom Mtns

Dublin/ Wicklow Mtns

Blackstairs Mtns

South Midlands

Comeragh Mtns
(& Monavullagh Mtns)

Galty Mtns

Knockmealdown Mtns

Boggeragh Mtns

Paps/Derrynasaggart Mtns

AN INTRODUCTION TO MOUNTAINVIEWS.IE

First steps

Just over a decade ago anyone interested in hillwalking in Ireland would have needed to equip themselves with a small library of books to begin to explore all of the hills and mountains of Ireland. Some books dealt with summits above a certain height, others with mountains in a particular area or some simply enlightened the reader on the particular author's favourite or recommended walks. There was no resource available that provided a comprehensive list of all the summits on the island and how best to tackle them.

What was needed was a national means of collaborating to create detailed information on all mountain areas and other vital information like rights of way or difficulty levels of a particular walk or climb. Ireland had no resource of this nature though there were some useful foundations, such as the 600m list by the late Joss Lynam.

So, just over ten years ago, Simon Stewart sought to change all that, when he conceived the idea of MountainViews.ie. A hillwalking enthusiast since the 1970s, Simon also possessed the requisite skills to develop the website that was sorely lacking for Irish walkers. People who signed up to MountainViews.ie were invited to add to the collective knowledge contained on the site. As word spread of the substantial hillwalking resource available free of charge, those first few tentative steps soon became a continuous march of sharing.

Peak performance

A decade on, MountainViews.ie contains over 5,000 comments on 1,057 hills or mountains. Each top has its own separate page, which provides vital information for the hillwalker, everything from how to access the mountain, whether it can be climbed as part of a longer walk, or even suggestions as to where to park. Whether you want to find places to walk near where you live or explore areas in another part of the island, MountainViews.ie has information you can use. All of the information on the site is a collaborative effort on the part of MountainViews.ie members. With 60 to 100 new contributions each month, our knowledge of specific mountains or areas grows continuously and includes comments on local points of interest, personal stories about particular mountains, historic references and so on.

In March 2012 MountainViews introduced a track-sharing system that

A sample page of the MountainViews website

lets you see the exact routes taken by other members, recorded by GPS. After just four months in operation some 300 tracks had been added and with such support we anticipate offering a very useful library of options for walkers in the coming years.

The most recent feature, known as 'MountainViews 2.0' combines summit and track information using modern mapping. The display shows both summits and routes to them on a 'zoomable' map with selectable layers from the Ordnance Survey, Open Street Map and Google. A click brings up user information on the summits or tracks.

The four corners of Ireland

MountainViews.ie is easy to navigate and you can quickly identify a mountain area near you or one that interests you. We have divided the upland areas of Ireland into 60 separate mountain regions, such as 'The Mournes' or 'The MacGillycuddy's Reeks', along with less well known areas, such as 'Slieve Miskish'. Using our overview maps you can easily see where these are in relation to your location, to other towns or cities and to major roads. You can then identify mountains within each area that might be of particular interest to you and quickly find out specific heights, grid references, the OS paper map on which it appears and other information you might need to ascend safely. And, increasingly, you can see other users' routes, as mentioned earlier.

All walks of life

One of the features of MountainViews.ie that has proven very popular is the opportunity to log publicly the mountains that you have climbed – ascending 10 mountains is sufficient to make a start in the MountainViews 'Hall of Fame'. But a majority are not summiteers and most walkers simply prefer the occasional outing to enjoy the pleasures of the wilds.

MountainViews.ie caters for a wide range – the casual walker, the dedicated peak bagger, the parent, the local trekking club, etc. All will find information that can be essential to an enjoyable and successful trip to Ireland's upland areas. The site also offers the chance to exchange views with other walkers through our forums or perhaps to ask advice from someone who may be familiar with a particular area. All in all, MountainViews.ie offers a way to interact nationally with everyone interested in hillwalking whether they be very experienced or a novice.

A personal note from Simon Stewart, founder of MountainViews.ie

Over a decade after the website's launch, I'm absolutely delighted that MountainViews.ie has progressed so well, and pleased that the site has provided a forum for all of the island's walkers to share their collective knowledge, which is precisely what I had hoped to achieve. And among the items not mentioned above are initiatives, such as the committee (now two years in existence), our monthly newsletter going out to 12,000 people, our public meetings, our prose and photos, our family of eight complementary summit lists, our expeditions, our summit ratings, our member surveys, and our collaborations with OSI, OSM, British list creators, the WAI and MI. And of course the publication of this book, which is a reflection of the level of interest the website has generated. Let me just say on behalf of the committee of MountainViews.ie that we use and work with MountainViews because we enjoy it and we invite you to use the website as a springboard to countless enjoyable hillwalking excursions.

SUMMITEERING

This book contains lists of summits and mountain areas in Ireland. While many will want to use such lists for general reference or finding places to walk, others may be interested in systematically visiting summits. This is called summiteering or 'bagging' and can be thought of as a type of game.

Apart from the satisfaction of visiting places, you will find that summiteering has many benefits, such as bringing you to new and different mountain ranges, visiting the often isolated and uncrowded peaks with novel views. You will be challenged by the need to plan efficient and different routes. Summiteering has conservation benefits because it encourages us away from overused summits to more sustainable walking in less frequented places.

Perhaps the most important milestone in the game of summiteering was when Sir Hugh Munro published his list of Scottish summits and outliers in 1891. Almost immediately people started to take an interest in systematically visiting what was on the list. In fact there were references to this from 1892 in the journal of the Scottish Mountaineering Club. Today over 5,000 people have completed the Munros with more than 200 finishing a year. It is a major asset to tourism in Scotland.

In Ireland, various lists have been published over the years. Some people have chosen to follow these collections, such as Joss Lynam's list of 600m summits (1997–2002) or that of Paddy Dillon in *The Mountains of Ireland* (1992). MountainViews has a family of lists designed to cater for different interests and Irish geography. Some follow the conventional format based on height, such as the 600m Vandeleur-Lynams, while some are innovations intended for people with less time, such as the 'Local Hundred' list.

MountainViews displays member ratings and climbs for each Irish summit. What many find striking is that most of the best-rated places, often in the west, south or north-west, are little visited. You may be familiar with what is available in the Mournes, Wicklow or areas like the Galtys; however, there is superb and often better walking in the westerly ranges in places like the Mweelrea Mountains, the Brandon Group, Achill/Corraun, North Mayo, the Cahas or the Bluestacks. Many of these have huge sea and wilderness views and rugged, interesting summits. For example, the Cahas (on the Beara Peninsula) rate highly by quality but come 40th in terms of members' climbs logged. Perhaps not surprising because of the travel distance for many but nevertheless a great area to visit. And summiteering can give you that extra push to get there.

Summiteering in Ireland is still in its infancy and it is hard to know how many have followed earlier lists. However, since MountainViews records what members have logged as climbed (since 2002), we can state that there has been a marked uptake in what we have seen.

By May 2004 some 135 people had made a start and by May 2012 the equivalent figure was 1,429.

	LOGGED 10	LOGGED 50	LOGGED 200
MAY 2004	135	33	2
MAY 2012	1,429	382	52

From 2009 MountainViews started issuing certificates to summiteers who have climbed all on a given list at an annual ceremony.

One of the certificates that MountainViews gives out for completing a list, in this case the Local Hundred

Soulless ticking?

E. Moss, writing in 1952 about peak-bagging, stated: 'To those who prefer the dull routine of well-remembered and too-often-accomplished ascents, the peak-bagger is one who dashes soullessly from top to top and whose memory of the day can be summed-up in a tick on a list. But to me collecting tops in a list provides a framework for widening experience in the fascination of fresh country, unknown hills, and other natural beauties.'

Given that there always were good reasons for peak-bagging other than ticking lists, MountainViews has used the modern means of a website to further broaden peak-bagging, to enhance the 'framework' Moss referred to. This makes it easier for people to describe places in prose and photography, to learn about where they are walking and the place names, to make it more social, to share routes, etc. And our name for this richer activity is summiteering. We invite you to try it at whatever pace you want and with whatever target list and to share what you find with fellow members.

How to start

Log what you have climbed already at MountainViews.ie. You may be surprised at what you have already achieved. Pick a list that suits you. To start, this might be the 'Local Hundred' or the 'County Highpoints'. When you have opportunities to go out, perhaps with a club or with friends, read up about where you will be and use the occasion to visit summits on your list. Mark them as climbed (and any others not on your target list). After a while you will be able to see what you have done and also compare your progress with others on the 'Rising Summiteers' list. View what other people have found on the summits you have visited and perhaps write your own experiences.

Éanna Ní Lamhna, noted naturalist and broadcaster, receiving her award for climbing the County Highpoints of Ireland in 2012. (Currently she is working through her 'Local Hundred' and has done over half of these.)

THE VANDELEUR-LYNAM & ARDERIN LISTS

The Vandeleur-Lynam list includes Irish mountains with a height of at least 600m and a drop or prominence of at least 15m. The Arderin list includes those with a height of 500m and a prominence of 30m. (Drop or prominence is the height of a summit above the highest col to the nearest more prominent summit.)

Origins of the lists

The original version of MountainViews.ie and its list was developed in spring 2002. The publisher, Simon Stewart, saw it as a place for people to discuss walking in the hills, structured round a list of summits.

MountainViews started with a combined list of 500m and 600m summits, all used with the authors' permission. The 500m summits came from the list of Myrddyn Phillips and Michael Dewey (which includes all summits from 500m upwards with a 30m prominence). The 600m summits came from the list issued by the late Joss Lynam in 1999 (with 15m prominence) modified by two sets of corrections from Joss (see Appendix). The summits from 600 to 609m drew data from both Joss Lynam and the Phillips/Dewey sources.

The original MountainViews list, like all lists of the period, had many limitations; however, as MountainViews attracted interest and members, many of the issues have been addressed. These issues have included:

▲ Finding proper historical and Irish names for the summits.

▲ Creating and reorganising *c.* 60 proper area and further sub-area names.

▲ Checking and adding geographical information such as height, prominence and isolation.

▲ Establishing where the tops are with member-supplied GPS and Abney Level measurements.

▲ Adding basic supplementary information such as name origins, county names, longitude and latitude, OS map sheet, derived geographical information and height ranking.

▲ Providing tools for members to indicate what they have logged and to assess each summit in seven categories, e.g. Challenge, View and Access.

▲ Adding and then refining user information and experience. This has included some 5,500 trip reports, informative articles and over 4,000 photographs.

In 2009 MountainViews took a long, hard look at what would make sense as a complete family of lists, introducing such list names as Arderin,Vandeleur-Lynam, Binnions and County Highpoints.

In late 2009 MountainViews discussed with Joss Lynam what the ongoing specification for the Vandeleur-Lynam list should be, as part of a continuing discussion in the general area (see Appendix).

A family of lists

MountainViews believes that Ireland is best served by a range of lists suitable for the range of interests of users and has come up with a family of lists for this purpose.

Some people are looking for a lifetime challenge done over many years. There are those, often at a time-poor stage of life, who want shorter, more quickly achieved challenges. Many are not interested in any challenge and simply want described places to walk, whether local or at a visit destination. To meet these diverse ends MountainViews offers a selection of lists:

Quicker-to-complete lists:

▲ The County Highpoints
The 27 highest points, some shared and some not necessarily summits, of the 32 counties of Ireland.

▲ The Local Hundred
The 100 summits nearest to where a member states he or she is based.

▲ The 900s
For Ireland these happen to be the same fourteen 900m summits that constitute the 3,000-footers.

▲ The Hundred Highest
100m prominence. A plain list of the Hundred Highest requires visiting 21 mountain areas. However, the MountainViews list with the prominence requirement of 100m spreads the selection over a more interesting 30, which is about half the full number of mountain areas.

▲ The Best 100
From accumulated ratings by members. Although based on members' subjective assessments, after thousands of ratings the resulting list has proved remarkably stable. Many visitors to Ireland have commented favourably on the value of this list to them in providing a target.

Longer-to-complete lists:

▲ The Vandeleur-Lynam List

The traditional Irish-sourced list with 269 summits of 600m+ and 15m prominence

▲ The Arderins

404 summits of 500m+ and 30m prominence. (Those over 600m also appear in the V-L list.)

▲ The Carns

335 summits of 400m to 499m with 30m prominence

▲ The Binnions

211 tops of 150m to 399m with 150m prominence

It is usually convenient to pick off some of the smaller tops as you work through higher summits.

A mountain or a hill?

MountainViews holds that mountains in the Irish context start at 500m.

Origin of the name: looking north from Arderin, at 527m the highest summit in the Slieve Bloom Mountains

EXPLANATION OF FIELDS

Note: An asterisk (*) in any field denotes updated or revised data by Mountainviews.ie

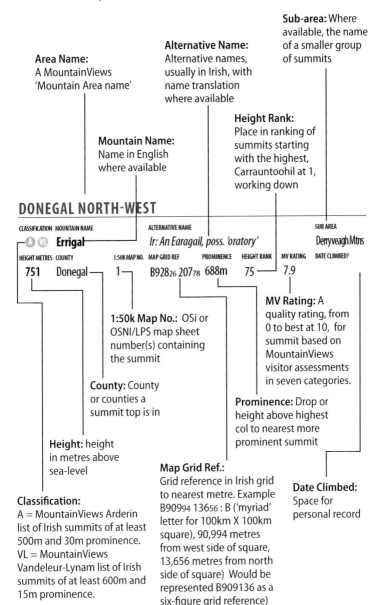

Sub-area: Where available, the name of a smaller group of summits

Alternative Name: Alternative names, usually in Irish, with name translation where available

Area Name: A MountainViews 'Mountain Area name'

Height Rank: Place in ranking of summits starting with the highest, Carrauntoohil at 1, working down

Mountain Name: Name in English where available

DONEGAL NORTH-WEST

CLASSIFICATION	MOUNTAIN NAME		ALTERNATIVE NAME			SUB AREA
Ⓐ ⓋⓁ	**Errigal**		*Ir: An Earagail, poss. 'oratory'*			Derryveagh Mtns

HEIGHT METRES	COUNTY	1:50K MAP NO.	MAP GRID REF	PROMINENCE	HEIGHT RANK	MV RATING	DATE CLIMBED?
751	Donegal	1	B928₂₆ 207₇₈	688m	75	7.9	

MV Rating: A quality rating, from 0 to best at 10, for summit based on MountainViews visitor assessments in seven categories.

1:50k Map No.: OSi or OSNI/LPS map sheet number(s) containing the summit

County: County or counties a summit top is in

Prominence: Drop or height above highest col to nearest more prominent summit

Height: height in metres above sea-level

Map Grid Ref.: Grid reference in Irish grid to nearest metre. Example B909₉₄ 136₅₆ : B ('myriad' letter for 100km X 100km square), 90,994 metres from west side of square, 13,656 metres from north side of square) Would be represented B909136 as a six-figure grid reference)

Date Climbed: Space for personal record

Classification: A = MountainViews Arderin list of Irish summits of at least 500m and 30m prominence. VL = MountainViews Vandeleur-Lynam list of Irish summits of at least 600m and 15m prominence.

Corraun Hill East Top and the north-facing corries

ACHILL AND THE CORRAUN PENINSULA

CLASSIFICATION	MOUNTAIN NAME	ALTERNATIVE NAME					SUB-AREA
Ⓐ ⓋⓁ	**Croaghan**	*Ir: Cruachán, 'little stack'*					Achill Island
HEIGHT METRES	COUNTY	1:50K MAP NO.	MAP GRID REF	PROMINENCE	HEIGHT RANK	MV RATING	DATE CLIMBED
688m	Mayo	22/30	F 599₆₂ 060₉₁	688m	124	9.4	

CLASSIFICATION	MOUNTAIN NAME	ALTERNATIVE NAME					SUB-AREA
Ⓐ ⓋⓁ	**Slievemore**	*Ir: An Sliabh Mór, 'the big mountain'*					Achill Island
HEIGHT METRES	COUNTY	1:50K MAP NO.	MAP GRID REF	PROMINENCE	HEIGHT RANK	MV RATING	DATE CLIMBED
671m	Mayo	22/30	F650₃₇ 086₆₉	582m	1149	8.5	

CLASSIFICATION	MOUNTAIN NAME	ALTERNATIVE NAME					SUB-AREA
Ⓐ ⓋⓁ	**Croaghan SW Top**	*Ir: Cruachán, 'little stack'*					Achill Island
HEIGHT METRES	COUNTY	1:50K MAP NO.	MAP GRID REF	PROMINENCE	HEIGHT RANK	MV RATING	DATE CLIMBED
664	Mayo	22/30	F553₆₅ 058₄₃	39m	162	9.5	

CLASSIFICATION	MOUNTAIN NAME	ALTERNATIVE NAME					SUB-AREA
Ⓐ	**Corraun Hill E Top**	*Ir: Cnoc an Chorráin, 'hill of the hook'*					Corraun
HEIGHT METRES	COUNTY	1:50K MAP NO.	MAP GRID REF	PROMINENCE	HEIGHT RANK	MV RATING	DATE CLIMBED
541	Mayo	30	L777₃₇ 961₁₈	506m	364	9.0	

CLASSIFICATION	MOUNTAIN NAME	ALTERNATIVE NAME					SUB-AREA
Ⓐ	**Corraun Hill**	*Ir: Cnoc an Chorráin, 'hill of the hook'*					Corraun
HEIGHT METRES	COUNTY	1:50K MAP NO.	MAP GRID REF	PROMINENCE	HEIGHT RANK	MV RATING	DATE CLIMBED
524	Mayo	30	L754₀₆ 960₄₈	103m	397	8.0	

THE ANTRIM HILLS

Knocklayd and Rathlin Island from Slieveanorra summit

BALLYHOURA MOUNTAINS

CLASSIFICATION	MOUNTAIN NAME	ALTERNATIVE NAME				SUB-AREA	
Ⓐ	**Seefin Mtn W Top**	*Ir: Suí Finn, 'Fionn's seat'*					

HEIGHT METRES	COUNTY	1:50K MAP NO.	MAP GRID REF	PROMINENCE	HEIGHT RANK	MV RATING	DATE CLIMBED
528	Limerick	73	R644$_{54}$ 180$_{70}$	383m	389	6.5	

CLASSIFICATION	MOUNTAIN NAME	ALTERNATIVE NAME				SUB-AREA	
Ⓐ	**Seefin Mtn E Top**	*Ir: Suí Finn, 'Fionn's seat'*					

HEIGHT METRES	COUNTY	1:50K MAP NO.	MAP GRID REF	PROMINENCE	HEIGHT RANK	MV RATING	DATE CLIMBED
510	Limerick	73	R653$_{10}$ 179$_{34}$	35m	426	6.6	

Taking the track to Seefin from Long Hill in the Ballyhouras

Looking north-west to Ben Gorm and Killary Harbour from Devilsmother

BEN GORM MOUNTAINS

CLASSIFICATION	MOUNTAIN NAME	ALTERNATIVE NAME					SUB-AREA
Ⓐ ⓋⓁ	**Ben Gorm**	*Ir: An Bhinn Ghorm, 'the blue peak'*					

HEIGHT METRES	COUNTY	1:50K MAP NO.	MAP GRID REF	PROMINENCE	HEIGHT RANK	MV RATING	DATE CLIMBED
700	Mayo	37	L861₈₄ 652₃₃	670m	109	9.5	

CLASSIFICATION	MOUNTAIN NAME	ALTERNATIVE NAME					SUB-AREA
Ⓐ ⓋⓁ	**Ben Creggan**	*Ir: Binn an Chreagáin, 'peak of the rocky patch'*					

HEIGHT METRES	COUNTY	1:50K MAP NO.	MAP GRID REF	PROMINENCE	HEIGHT RANK	MV RATING	DATE CLIMBED
693	Mayo	37	L857₀₉ 666₀₄	88m	116	8.6	

CLASSIFICATION	MOUNTAIN NAME	ALTERNATIVE NAME					SUB-AREA
Ⓐ ⓋⓁ	**Ben Creggan S Top**	*Ir: Meall Láir, 'middle lump'*					

HEIGHT METRES	COUNTY	1:50K MAP NO.	MAP GRID REF	PROMINENCE	HEIGHT RANK	MV RATING	DATE CLIMBED
687	Mayo	37	L858₄₆ 661₀₂	72m	125	7.8	

BLACKSTAIRS MOUNTAINS

CLASSIFICATION	MOUNTAIN NAME	ALTERNATIVE NAME					SUB-AREA
A VL	**Mount Leinster**	*Ir: Stua Laighean, 'prince (or warrior) of Leinster'*					
HEIGHT METRES	COUNTY	1:50K MAP NO.	MAP GRID REF	PROMINENCE	HEIGHT RANK	MV RATING	DATE CLIMBED
795	Carlow/Wexford	68	S826 03 526 08	707m	43	7.8	

CLASSIFICATION	MOUNTAIN NAME	ALTERNATIVE NAME					SUB-AREA
A VL	**Blackstairs Mtn**	*Ir: na Staighrí Dubha, 'the black stairs'*					
HEIGHT METRES	COUNTY	1:50K MAP NO.	MAP GRID REF	PROMINENCE	HEIGHT RANK	MV RATING	DATE CLIMBED
735	Carlow/Wexford	68	S810 59 448 33	540m	84	8.1	

CLASSIFICATION	MOUNTAIN NAME	ALTERNATIVE NAME					SUB-AREA
VL	**Mount Leinster E Top**	*Ir: Stua Laighean, 'prince (or warrior) of Leinster'*					
HEIGHT METRES	COUNTY	1:50K MAP NO.	MAP GRID REF	PROMINENCE	HEIGHT RANK	MV RATING	DATE CLIMBED
654	Wexford	68	S844 46 527 80	29m	180	8.0	

CLASSIFICATION	MOUNTAIN NAME	ALTERNATIVE NAME					SUB-AREA
A	**Knockroe**	*Ir: Cnoc Rua, 'red hill'*					
HEIGHT METRES	COUNTY	1:50K MAP NO.	MAP GRID REF	PROMINENCE	HEIGHT RANK	MV RATING	DATE CLIMBED
540	Carlow	68	S819 50 496 38	95m	368	7.4	

CLASSIFICATION	MOUNTAIN NAME	ALTERNATIVE NAME					SUB-AREA
A	**Slievebawn**	*Ir: Sliabh Bán, 'white mountain'*					
HEIGHT METRES	COUNTY	1:50K MAP NO.	MAP GRID REF	PROMINENCE	HEIGHT RANK	MV RATING	DATE CLIMBED
520	Carlow	68	S806 36 548 17	85m	404	7.1	

CLASSIFICATION	MOUNTAIN NAME	ALTERNATIVE NAME					SUB-AREA
A	**Bran Scultair**						
HEIGHT METRES	COUNTY	1:50K MAP NO.	MAP GRID REF	PROMINENCE	HEIGHT RANK	MV RATING	DATE CLIMBED
504	Carlow/Wexford	68	S785 98 400 81	129m	440	7.0	

Slievebawn summit cairn, with Knockroe and Blackstairs in the distance

BLUESTACK MOUNTAINS

CLASSIFICATION	MOUNTAIN NAME	ALTERNATIVE NAME			SUB-AREA
Ⓐ Ⓥ	**Croaghgorm**	*Ir: An Chruach Ghorm, 'the blue stack'*			

HEIGHT METRES	COUNTY	1:50K MAP NO.	MAP GRID REF	PROMINENCE	HEIGHT RANK	MV RATING	DATE CLIMBED
674	Donegal	11	G948₃₂ 895₈₅	541m	146	9.0	

CLASSIFICATION	MOUNTAIN NAME	ALTERNATIVE NAME			SUB-AREA
Ⓐ Ⓥ	**Lavagh More**	*Ir: An Leamhach Mhór, poss. 'big place of elms'*			

HEIGHT METRES	COUNTY	1:50K MAP NO.	MAP GRID REF	PROMINENCE	HEIGHT RANK	MV RATING	DATE CLIMBED
671	Donegal	11	G935₃₁ 910₁₀	193m	150	9.2	

CLASSIFICATION	MOUNTAIN NAME	ALTERNATIVE NAME			SUB-AREA
Ⓐ Ⓥ	**Lavagh Beg**	*Ir: An Leamhach Bheag, poss. 'little place of elms'*			

HEIGHT METRES	COUNTY	1:50K MAP NO.	MAP GRID REF	PROMINENCE	HEIGHT RANK	MV RATING	DATE CLIMBED
650	Donegal	11	G926₂₄ 915₃₆	93m	190	8.0	

CLASSIFICATION	MOUNTAIN NAME	ALTERNATIVE NAME			SUB-AREA
Ⓐ Ⓥ	**Ardnageer**	*Ir: Ard na gCaor, 'height of the berries'*			

HEIGHT METRES	COUNTY	1:50K MAP NO.	MAP GRID REF	PROMINENCE	HEIGHT RANK	MV RATING	DATE CLIMBED
642	Donegal	11	G969₆₉ 908₉₈	77m	199	9.2	

Lough Belshade in the Bluestacks

Looking from Gaugin south to Croaghbane, across the Polldoo Glen

CLASSIFICATION	MOUNTAIN NAME	ALTERNATIVE NAME		SUB-AREA
Ⓐ Ⓥ	**Croaghbane**	*Ir: An Chruach Bhán, 'white stack'*		

HEIGHT METRES	COUNTY	1:50K MAP NO.	MAP GRID REF	PROMINENCE	HEIGHT RANK	MV RATING	DATE CLIMBED
641	Donegal	11	G978₅₁ 910₇₂	76m	203	8.3	

CLASSIFICATION	MOUNTAIN NAME	ALTERNATIVE NAME		SUB-AREA
Ⓥ	**Ardnageer SW Top**	*Ir: Ard na gCaor, 'height of the berries'*		

HEIGHT METRES	COUNTY	1:50K MAP NO.	MAP GRID REF	PROMINENCE	HEIGHT RANK	MV RATING	DATE CLIMBED
626	Donegal	11	G963₃₂ 904₈₅	21m	229	9.1	

CLASSIFICATION	MOUNTAIN NAME	ALTERNATIVE NAME		SUB-AREA
Ⓐ Ⓥ	**Silver Hill**	*Ir: Cruach an Airgid, 'stack of the silver'*		

HEIGHT METRES	COUNTY	1:50K MAP NO.	MAP GRID REF	PROMINENCE	HEIGHT RANK	MV RATING	DATE CLIMBED
600	Donegal	11	G906₅₅ 912₈₁	155m	269	7.7	

CLASSIFICATION	MOUNTAIN NAME	ALTERNATIVE NAME		SUB-AREA
Ⓐ	**Aghla Mountain**	*Ir: An Eachla, poss. 'look-out point/prospect'*		

HEIGHT METRES	COUNTY	1:50K MAP NO.	MAP GRID REF	PROMINENCE	HEIGHT RANK	MV RATING	DATE CLIMBED
593	Donegal	11	G896₉₂ 988₉₅	388m	280	8.6	

Gaugin Mountain from the north

CLASSIFICATION	MOUNTAIN NAME		ALTERNATIVE NAME			SUB-AREA	
Ⓐ	**Croaghnageer**		*Ir: Cruach na gCaor, 'stack of the berries'*				
HEIGHT METRES	COUNTY	1:50K MAP NO.	MAP GRID REF	PROMINENCE	HEIGHT RANK	MV RATING	DATE CLIMBED
571	Donegal	11	H011₃₅ 886₄₃	266m	318	8.8	

CLASSIFICATION	MOUNTAIN NAME		ALTERNATIVE NAME			SUB-AREA	
Ⓐ	**Gaugin Mountain**		*Ir: An Gáigín, 'the little cleft'*				
HEIGHT METRES	COUNTY	1:50K MAP NO.	MAP GRID REF	PROMINENCE	HEIGHT RANK	MV RATING	DATE CLIMBED
565	Donegal	6/11	G983₂₃ 949₉₉	290m	327	7.7	

CLASSIFICATION	MOUNTAIN NAME		ALTERNATIVE NAME			SUB-AREA	
Ⓐ	**Croaghanirwore**		*Ir: Cruach an Fhir Mhóir, 'stack of the big man'*				
HEIGHT METRES	COUNTY	1:50K MAP NO.	MAP GRID REF	PROMINENCE	HEIGHT RANK	MV RATING	DATE CLIMBED
548	Donegal	11	H002₂₆ 892₀₆	93m	355	8.8	

CLASSIFICATION	MOUNTAIN NAME		ALTERNATIVE NAME			SUB-AREA	
Ⓐ	**Croaghconnellagh**		*Ir: Cruach Conallach, 'stack of the Cenél Conaill'*				
HEIGHT METRES	COUNTY	1:50K MAP NO.	MAP GRID REF	PROMINENCE	HEIGHT RANK	MV RATING	DATE CLIMBED
523	Donegal	11	H023₀₀ 863₀₀	268m	400	7.5	

CLASSIFICATION	MOUNTAIN NAME		ALTERNATIVE NAME			SUB-AREA	
Ⓐ	**Carnaween**		*Ir: Carn na nÉan, 'cairn of the birds'*				
HEIGHT METRES	COUNTY	1:50K MAP NO.	MAP GRID REF	PROMINENCE	HEIGHT RANK	MV RATING	DATE CLIMBED
521	Donegal	11	G875₉₈ 891₅₁	166m	401	8.4	

CLASSIFICATION	MOUNTAIN NAME		ALTERNATIVE NAME			SUB-AREA	
Ⓐ	**Binasruell**		*Ir: Binn na Sruthal, 'peak of the streams'*				
HEIGHT METRES	COUNTY	1:50K MAP NO.	MAP GRID REF	PROMINENCE	HEIGHT RANK	MV RATING	DATE CLIMBED
505	Donegal	11	G918₃₉ 897₂₀	42m	438	8.0	

BOGGERAGH MOUNTAINS

CLASSIFICATION	MOUNTAIN NAME	ALTERNATIVE NAME				SUB-AREA
Ⓐ ⓋⓁ	**Musheramore**	*Ir: Muisire Mór, 'great (mountain) of the Múscraige'*				
HEIGHT METRES	COUNTY	1:50K MAP NO.	MAP GRID REF	PROMINENCE	HEIGHT RANK	MV RATING	DATE CLIMBED
644	Cork	79	W328₇₅ 850₄₇	439m	198	6.4	

Looking west from the summit of Musheramore

BRANDON GROUP

CLASSIFICATION	MOUNTAIN NAME	ALTERNATIVE NAME				SUB-AREA
Ⓐ ⓋⓁ	**Brandon**	*Ir: Cnoc Bréanainn, 'Brendan's hill'*				
HEIGHT METRES	COUNTY	1:50K MAP NO.	MAP GRID REF	PROMINENCE	HEIGHT RANK	MV RATING	DATE CLIMBED
951.7*	Kerry	70	Q460₄₂ 116₀₅	934m	9	8.6	

CLASSIFICATION	MOUNTAIN NAME	ALTERNATIVE NAME				SUB-AREA
ⓋⓁ	**Brandon Nth Top**	*Ir: Cnoc Bréanainn, 'Brendan's hill'*				
HEIGHT METRES	COUNTY	1:50K MAP NO.	MAP GRID REF	PROMINENCE	HEIGHT RANK	MV RATING	DATE CLIMBED
895.4*	Kerry	70	Q461₀₉ 125₄₁	23m	15	9.0	

CLASSIFICATION	MOUNTAIN NAME	ALTERNATIVE NAME				SUB-AREA
Ⓐ ⓋⓁ	**Brandon Peak**	*Ir: Barr an Ghéaráin, 'top of the fang'*				
HEIGHT METRES	COUNTY	1:50K MAP NO.	MAP GRID REF	PROMINENCE	HEIGHT RANK	MV RATING	DATE CLIMBED
840	Kerry	70	Q472₀₇ 094₈₁	190m	24	9.1	

CLASSIFICATION	MOUNTAIN NAME	ALTERNATIVE NAME				SUB-AREA
Ⓐ ⓋⓁ	**Benagh**	*Ir: Binn Faiche, 'peak of Faha'*				
HEIGHT METRES	COUNTY	1:50K MAP NO.	MAP GRID REF	PROMINENCE	HEIGHT RANK	MV RATING	DATE CLIMBED
822	Kerry	70	Q469₀₈ 119₂₈	57m	30	9.1	

CLASSIFICATION	MOUNTAIN NAME	ALTERNATIVE NAME				SUB-AREA
Ⓐ ⓋⓁ	**Faha Ridge**	*Ir: Na Poirt, 'the fortifications'*				
HEIGHT METRES	COUNTY	1:50K MAP NO.	MAP GRID REF	PROMINENCE	HEIGHT RANK	MV RATING	DATE CLIMBED
809	Kerry	70	Q464₃₆ 120₅₀	44m	34	9.2	

CLASSIFICATION	MOUNTAIN NAME		ALTERNATIVE NAME				SUB-AREA
ⓋⓁ	**Gearhane**		*Ir: An Géarán, 'the fang'*				

HEIGHT METRES	COUNTY	1:50K MAP NO.	MAP GRID REF	PROMINENCE	HEIGHT RANK	MV RATING	DATE CLIMBED
803	Kerry	70	Q468₂₅ 087₉₃ 18m		36	9.2	

CLASSIFICATION	MOUNTAIN NAME		ALTERNATIVE NAME				SUB-AREA
ⓋⓁ	**Brandon Sth Top**		*Ir: Faill na nDeamhan, 'cliff of the demons'*				

HEIGHT METRES	COUNTY	1:50K MAP NO.	MAP GRID REF	PROMINENCE	HEIGHT RANK	MV RATING	DATE CLIMBED
790	Kerry	70	Q468₃₆ 107₀₄ 25m		48	9.4	

CLASSIFICATION	MOUNTAIN NAME		ALTERNATIVE NAME				SUB-AREA
Ⓐ ⓋⓁ	**Masatiompan**		*Ir: Más an Tiompáin, 'rump of the drum/hump/hollow'*				

HEIGHT METRES	COUNTY	1:50K MAP NO.	MAP GRID REF	PROMINENCE	HEIGHT RANK	MV RATING	DATE CLIMBED
763	Kerry	70	Q465₃₂ 145₅₄ 108m		65	9.4	

CLASSIFICATION	MOUNTAIN NAME		ALTERNATIVE NAME				SUB-AREA
Ⓐ ⓋⓁ	**Pierasmore**		*Ir: Piaras Mór, 'big [obscure element]'*				

HEIGHT METRES	COUNTY	1:50K MAP NO.	MAP GRID REF	PROMINENCE	HEIGHT RANK	MV RATING	DATE CLIMBED
748	Kerry	70	Q463₈₀ 136₅₅ 33m		76	8.9	

CLASSIFICATION	MOUNTAIN NAME		ALTERNATIVE NAME				SUB-AREA
Ⓐ ⓋⓁ	**Ballysitteragh**		*Ir: An Scraig, 'rocky outcrop'*				

HEIGHT METRES	COUNTY	1:50K MAP NO.	MAP GRID REF	PROMINENCE	HEIGHT RANK	MV RATING	DATE CLIMBED
623	Kerry	70	Q460₅₅ 057₂₁ 218m		232	8.1	

CLASSIFICATION	MOUNTAIN NAME		ALTERNATIVE NAME				SUB-AREA
ⓋⓁ	**Beennabrack**		*Ir: Macha na gCab, 'plain of the beaks'*				

HEIGHT METRES	COUNTY	1:50K MAP NO.	MAP GRID REF	PROMINENCE	HEIGHT RANK	MV RATING	DATE CLIMBED
608.5*	Kerry	70	Q468₆₅ 053₇₂ 23m		251	7.1	

Approaching the rocky knoll of Pierasmore

Next stop America: west from Masatiompan

The Faha Ridge on Brandon

Facing west along Cuilcagh's ridge from near the summit

BREIFNE

CLASSIFICATION	MOUNTAIN NAME		ALTERNATIVE NAME				SUB-AREA
A VL	**Cuilcagh**		*Ir: Binn Chuilceach, 'chalky peak'*				Cuilcagh Mtns
HEIGHT METRES	COUNTY	1:50K MAP NO.	MAP GRID REF	PROMINENCE	HEIGHT RANK	MV RATING	DATE CLIMBED
665	Cavan/Fermanagh	26/27A	H123$_{56}$ 280$_{17}$	570m	161	8.3	

CLASSIFICATION	MOUNTAIN NAME		ALTERNATIVE NAME				SUB-AREA
A	**Slieve Anierin**		*Ir: Sliabh an Iarainn, 'mountain of the iron'*				Iron Mtns
HEIGHT METRES	COUNTY	1:50K MAP NO.	MAP GRID REF	PROMINENCE	HEIGHT RANK	MV RATING	DATE CLIMBED
585	Leitrim	26	H018$_{78}$ 159$_{30}$	245m	296	7.4	

CLASSIFICATION	MOUNTAIN NAME		ALTERNATIVE NAME				SUB-AREA
A	**Knockacullion**		*Knockabell*				Iron Mtns
HEIGHT METRES	COUNTY	1:50K MAP NO.	MAP GRID REF	PROMINENCE	HEIGHT RANK	MV RATING	DATE CLIMBED
562	Leitrim	26	H030$_{59}$ 177$_{91}$	57m	330	7.2	

CLASSIFICATION	MOUNTAIN NAME		ALTERNATIVE NAME				SUB-AREA
A	**Slievenakilla**		*The Playbank or The Playground*				Cuilcagh Mtns
HEIGHT METRES	COUNTY	1:50K MAP NO.	MAP GRID REF	PROMINENCE	HEIGHT RANK	MV RATING	DATE CLIMBED
542	Cavan	26	H033$_{00}$ 258$_{00}$	187m	362	6.7	

CLASSIFICATION	MOUNTAIN NAME		ALTERNATIVE NAME				SUB-AREA
A	**Benbeg**		*Ir: Binn Bheag, 'little peak'*				Cuilcagh Mtns
HEIGHT METRES	COUNTY	1:50K MAP NO.	MAP GRID REF	PROMINENCE	HEIGHT RANK	MV RATING	DATE CLIMBED
539	Cavan	26/27A	H120$_{87}$ 254$_{26}$	34m	370	7.0	

CLASSIFICATION	MOUNTAIN NAME		ALTERNATIVE NAME				SUB-AREA
Ⓐ	**Bencroy**		Ir: Gob na bhFiach, 'point/beak of the ravens'				Iron Mtns

HEIGHT METRES	COUNTY	1:50K MAP NO.	MAP GRID REF	PROMINENCE	HEIGHT RANK	MV RATING	DATE CLIMBED
518	Leitrim	26	H045$_{54}$ 190$_{83}$ 83m		408	7.4	

CLASSIFICATION	MOUNTAIN NAME		ALTERNATIVE NAME				SUB-AREA
Ⓐ	**Benbrack**		Ir: An Bhinn Bhreac, 'the speckled peak'				Cuilcagh Mtns

HEIGHT METRES	COUNTY	1:50K MAP NO.	MAP GRID REF	PROMINENCE	HEIGHT RANK	MV RATING	DATE CLIMBED
502	Cavan	26/27A	H101$_{17}$ 216$_{00}$ 147m		444	7.6	

CAHA MOUNTAINS

CLASSIFICATION	MOUNTAIN NAME		ALTERNATIVE NAME				SUB-AREA
Ⓐ Ⓥ	**Hungry Hill**		Ir: Cnoc Daod, 'hill of the tooth/set of teeth'				

HEIGHT METRES	COUNTY	1:50K MAP NO.	MAP GRID REF	PROMINENCE	HEIGHT RANK	MV RATING	DATE CLIMBED
685	Cork	84	V760$_{88}$ 497$_{26}$ 400m		127	8.9	

CLASSIFICATION	MOUNTAIN NAME		ALTERNATIVE NAME				SUB-AREA
Ⓐ Ⓥ	**Knockowen**		Ir: Cnoc Eoghain, 'hill of Eoghan'				

HEIGHT METRES	COUNTY	1:50K MAP NO.	MAP GRID REF	PROMINENCE	HEIGHT RANK	MV RATING	DATE CLIMBED
658	Cork/Kerry	84	V808$_{70}$ 553$_{93}$ 373m		171	8.7	

CLASSIFICATION	MOUNTAIN NAME		ALTERNATIVE NAME				SUB-AREA
Ⓐ Ⓥ	**Coomnadiha**		Ir: Com na Daibhche, 'hollow of the hole'				

HEIGHT METRES	COUNTY	1:50K MAP NO.	MAP GRID REF	PROMINENCE	HEIGHT RANK	MV RATING	DATE CLIMBED
644	Kerry	85	V847$_{29}$ 600$_{38}$ 209m		197	8.1	

CLASSIFICATION	MOUNTAIN NAME		ALTERNATIVE NAME				SUB-AREA
Ⓐ Ⓥ	**Maulin**		Ir: Málainn, meaning obscure				

HEIGHT METRES	COUNTY	1:50K MAP NO.	MAP GRID REF	PROMINENCE	HEIGHT RANK	MV RATING	DATE CLIMBED
621	Cork	84	V712$_{90}$ 505$_{30}$ 226m		234	8.6	

CLASSIFICATION	MOUNTAIN NAME		ALTERNATIVE NAME				SUB-AREA
Ⓐ Ⓥ	**Lackabane**		Ir: An Leaca Bhán, 'the white hillside'				

HEIGHT METRES	COUNTY	1:50K MAP NO.	MAP GRID REF	PROMINENCE	HEIGHT RANK	MV RATING	DATE CLIMBED
602	Kerry	84	V751$_{48}$ 536$_{95}$ 287m		261	9.8	

CLASSIFICATION	MOUNTAIN NAME		ALTERNATIVE NAME				SUB-AREA
Ⓐ Ⓥ	**Eskatarriff**		Ir: Eisc an Tairbh, 'ravine of the bull'				

HEIGHT METRES	COUNTY	1:50K MAP NO.	MAP GRID REF	PROMINENCE	HEIGHT RANK	MV RATING	DATE CLIMBED
600	Cork/Kerry	84	V736$_{48}$ 533$_{18}$ 135m		266	8.2	

CLASSIFICATION	MOUNTAIN NAME		ALTERNATIVE NAME				SUB-AREA
Ⓐ	**Coomacloghane**		Ir: Com an Chlocháin, 'hollow of the stone building'				

HEIGHT METRES	COUNTY	1:50K MAP NO.	MAP GRID REF	PROMINENCE	HEIGHT RANK	MV RATING	DATE CLIMBED
599	Cork/Kerry	84	V732$_{77}$ 548$_{24}$ 104m		270	9.1	

CLASSIFICATION	MOUNTAIN NAME		ALTERNATIVE NAME				SUB-AREA
Ⓐ	**Cushnaficulla**		*Ir: Cois na Fiacaile, 'beside the tooth'*				

HEIGHT METRES	COUNTY	1:50K MAP NO.	MAP GRID REF	PROMINENCE	HEIGHT RANK	MV RATING	DATE CLIMBED
594	Cork/Kerry	84	V821$_{78}$ 559$_{06}$	59m	278	8.6	

CLASSIFICATION	MOUNTAIN NAME		ALTERNATIVE NAME				SUB-AREA
Ⓐ	**Tooth Mtn**		*Ir: Cnoc na bhFiacal, 'hill of the teeth'*				

HEIGHT METRES	COUNTY	1:50K MAP NO.	MAP GRID REF	PROMINENCE	HEIGHT RANK	MV RATING	DATE CLIMBED
590	Kerry	84	V741$_{68}$ 553$_{66}$	45m	286	9.3	

CLASSIFICATION	MOUNTAIN NAME		ALTERNATIVE NAME				SUB-AREA
Ⓐ	**Knocknagree**		*Ir: Cnoc na Groí, 'hill of the horses'*				

HEIGHT METRES	COUNTY	1:50K MAP NO.	MAP GRID REF	PROMINENCE	HEIGHT RANK	MV RATING	DATE CLIMBED
586	Cork	84	V726$_{70}$ 505$_{67}$	131m	292	9.6	

CLASSIFICATION	MOUNTAIN NAME		ALTERNATIVE NAME				SUB-AREA
Ⓐ	**Knockeirky**						

HEIGHT METRES	COUNTY	1:50K MAP NO.	MAP GRID REF	PROMINENCE	HEIGHT RANK	MV RATING	DATE CLIMBED
577	Cork/Kerry	84	V832$_{15}$ 557$_{30}$	30m	308	9.0	

The ridge from Derryclancy to Hungry Hill

The distinctive white trig pillar at Sugarloaf's summit overlooking Bantry Bay

CLASSIFICATION	MOUNTAIN NAME		ALTERNATIVE NAME				SUB-AREA
Ⓐ	**Sugarloaf Mtn**		*Ir: Gabhal Mhór, 'big fork'*				
HEIGHT METRES	COUNTY	1:50K MAP NO.	MAP GRID REF	PROMINENCE	HEIGHT RANK	MV RATING	DATE CLIMBED
574	Cork	85	V873₇₇ 529₅₁	126m	311	9.1	

CLASSIFICATION	MOUNTAIN NAME		ALTERNATIVE NAME				SUB-AREA
Ⓐ	**Lackawee**		*Ir: An Leaca Bhuí, 'the yellow hillside'*				
HEIGHT METRES	COUNTY	1:50K MAP NO.	MAP GRID REF	PROMINENCE	HEIGHT RANK	MV RATING	DATE CLIMBED
572	Cork	84	V703₅₉ 517₂₂	67m	316	8.6	

CLASSIFICATION	MOUNTAIN NAME		ALTERNATIVE NAME				SUB-AREA
Ⓐ	**Sugarloaf Mtn W Top**		*Ir: Gabhal Mhór, 'big fork'*				
HEIGHT METRES	COUNTY	1:50K MAP NO.	MAP GRID REF	PROMINENCE	HEIGHT RANK	MV RATING	DATE CLIMBED
560	Cork	85	V861₂₉ 532₃₅	85m	334	8.0	

CLASSIFICATION	MOUNTAIN NAME		ALTERNATIVE NAME				SUB-AREA
Ⓐ	**Derryclancy**		*Doire Cluainsí, 'oak grove of [?] Cluainseach'*				
HEIGHT METRES	COUNTY	1:50K MAP NO.	MAP GRID REF	PROMINENCE	HEIGHT RANK	MV RATING	DATE CLIMBED
554	Cork/Kerry	84	V769₀₁ 513₂₅	109m	346	7.5	

CLASSIFICATION	MOUNTAIN NAME		ALTERNATIVE NAME				SUB-AREA
Ⓐ	**Killane Mtn**		*Ir: An Calán, 'gallon' or 'vessel'*				
HEIGHT METRES	COUNTY	1:50K MAP NO.	MAP GRID REF	PROMINENCE	HEIGHT RANK	MV RATING	DATE CLIMBED
537	Cork/Kerry	85	V872₉₀ 595₅₉	82m	371	8.6	

CLASSIFICATION	MOUNTAIN NAME		ALTERNATIVE NAME			SUB-AREA	
Ⓐ	**Eskatarriff E Top**		*Ir: Eisc an Tairbh, 'ravine of the bull'*				
HEIGHT METRES	COUNTY	1:50K MAP NO.	MAP GRID REF	PROMINENCE	HEIGHT RANK	MV RATING	DATE CLIMBED
531	Kerry	84	V742$_{92}$ 531$_{49}$	36m	383	9.1	

CLASSIFICATION	MOUNTAIN NAME		ALTERNATIVE NAME			SUB-AREA	
Ⓐ	**Nareera**						
HEIGHT METRES	COUNTY	1:50K MAP NO.	MAP GRID REF	PROMINENCE	HEIGHT RANK	MV RATING	DATE CLIMBED
530	Cork	85	V855$_{39}$ 531$_{72}$	35m	386	7.6	

CLASSIFICATION	MOUNTAIN NAME		ALTERNATIVE NAME			SUB-AREA	
Ⓐ	**Cummeenbaun**		*Ir: An Coimín Bán, 'the white little hollow'*				
HEIGHT METRES	COUNTY	1:50K MAP NO.	MAP GRID REF	PROMINENCE	HEIGHT RANK	MV RATING	DATE CLIMBED
510	Kerry	84	V823$_{21}$ 581$_{41}$	35m	424	6.8	

CLASSIFICATION	MOUNTAIN NAME		ALTERNATIVE NAME			SUB-AREA	
Ⓐ	**Knocknagorraveela**		*Ir: Cnoc na gCorrmhíolta, 'hill of the midges'*				
HEIGHT METRES	COUNTY	1:50K MAP NO.	MAP GRID REF	PROMINENCE	HEIGHT RANK	MV RATING	DATE CLIMBED
507	Kerry	85	V871$_{74}$ 625$_{20}$	152m	434	7.1	

CLASSIFICATION	MOUNTAIN NAME		ALTERNATIVE NAME			SUB-AREA	
Ⓐ	**Knockreagh**		*Ir: An Cnoc Riabhach, 'the grey/brindled hill'*				
HEIGHT METRES	COUNTY	1:50K MAP NO.	MAP GRID REF	PROMINENCE	HEIGHT RANK	MV RATING	DATE CLIMBED
500	Kerry	84	V826$_{98}$ 613$_{58}$	65m	451	7.6	

CENTRAL DINGLE

CLASSIFICATION	MOUNTAIN NAME		ALTERNATIVE NAME			SUB-AREA	
Ⓐ Ⓥ	**Beenoskee**		*Ir: Binn os Gaoith, 'mountain above the wind/estuary'*				
HEIGHT METRES	COUNTY	1:50K MAP NO.	MAP GRID REF	PROMINENCE	HEIGHT RANK	MV RATING	DATE CLIMBED
826	Kerry	70	Q580$_{62}$ 088$_{80}$	491m	28	8.9	

CLASSIFICATION	MOUNTAIN NAME		ALTERNATIVE NAME			SUB-AREA	
Ⓐ Ⓥ	**Stradbally Mtn**		*Ir: Cnoc an tSráidbhaile, 'hill of Stradbally'*				
HEIGHT METRES	COUNTY	1:50K MAP NO.	MAP GRID REF	PROMINENCE	HEIGHT RANK	MV RATING	DATE CLIMBED
798	Kerry	70	Q587$_{35}$ 091$_{47}$	40m	41	9.0	

CLASSIFICATION	MOUNTAIN NAME		ALTERNATIVE NAME			SUB-AREA	
Ⓐ Ⓥ	**Slieveanea NE Top**		*Ir: Sliabh Macha Ré, 'mountain of the smooth plain'*				
HEIGHT METRES	COUNTY	1:50K MAP NO.	MAP GRID REF	PROMINENCE	HEIGHT RANK	MV RATING	DATE CLIMBED
670	Kerry	70	Q515$_{80}$ 063$_{61}$	265m	151	8.5	

CLASSIFICATION	MOUNTAIN NAME		ALTERNATIVE NAME			SUB-AREA	
Ⓐ Ⓥ	**An Cnapán Mór**		*Gowlane Beg. Ir: An Cnapán Mór, 'the big lump'*				
HEIGHT METRES	COUNTY	1:50K MAP NO.	MAP GRID REF	PROMINENCE	HEIGHT RANK	MV RATING	DATE CLIMBED
649	Kerry	70	Q522$_{26}$ 045$_{91}$	81m	192	8.8	

CLASSIFICATION	MOUNTAIN NAME		ALTERNATIVE NAME			SUB-AREA	
Ⓐ Ⓥ	**Cnoc na Bánóige**		*Banoge Nth. Ir: Cnoc na Bánóige, 'hill of the grassy patch'*				
HEIGHT METRES	COUNTY	1:50K MAP NO.	MAP GRID REF	PROMINENCE	HEIGHT RANK	MV RATING	DATE CLIMBED
641	Kerry	70	Q548₂₇ 048₃₀	176m	201	9.0	

CLASSIFICATION	MOUNTAIN NAME		ALTERNATIVE NAME			SUB-AREA	
Ⓥ	**Slievanea**		*Ir: Sliabh Macha Ré, 'mountain of the smooth plain'*				
HEIGHT METRES	COUNTY	1:50K MAP NO.	MAP GRID REF	PROMINENCE	HEIGHT RANK	MV RATING	DATE CLIMBED
620	Kerry	70	Q507₄₈ 057₅₀	15m	236	9.1	

CLASSIFICATION	MOUNTAIN NAME		ALTERNATIVE NAME			SUB-AREA	
Ⓐ Ⓥ	**Coumbaun**		*Ir:An Com Bán, 'the white hollow'*				
HEIGHT METRES	COUNTY	1:50K MAP NO.	MAP GRID REF	PROMINENCE	HEIGHT RANK	MV RATING	DATE CLIMBED
610	Kerry	70	Q567₇₁ 091₉₂	42m	247	7.5	

CLASSIFICATION	MOUNTAIN NAME		ALTERNATIVE NAME			SUB-AREA	
Ⓐ	**Knockmulanane**		*Ir: Cnoc Mhaoilionáin, 'Mulfinan's hill'*				
HEIGHT METRES	COUNTY	1:50K MAP NO.	MAP GRID REF	PROMINENCE	HEIGHT RANK	MV RATING	DATE CLIMBED
593	Kerry	70	Q568₁₂ 048₇₈	48m	279	9.2	

The thin promontory of Croaghskearda overlooks Dingle Bay

CLASSIFICATION	MOUNTAIN NAME		ALTERNATIVE NAME				SUB-AREA
Ⓐ	**Beenatoor**		*Ir: Binn an Tuair, 'peak of the bleaching green'*				
HEIGHT METRES	COUNTY	1:50K MAP NO.	MAP GRID REF	PROMINENCE	HEIGHT RANK	MV RATING	DATE CLIMBED
592	Kerry	70	Q558₅₄ 089₀₇	66m	282	8.4	

CLASSIFICATION	MOUNTAIN NAME		ALTERNATIVE NAME				SUB-AREA
Ⓐ	**Dromavally Mtn**		*Ir: Cnoc Dhroim an Bhaile, 'hill of Dromavally'*				
HEIGHT METRES	COUNTY	1:50K MAP NO.	MAP GRID REF	PROMINENCE	HEIGHT RANK	MV RATING	DATE CLIMBED
552	Kerry	71	Q606₂₂ 066₄₆	206m	348	7.5	

COMERAGH MOUNTAINS

CLASSIFICATION	MOUNTAIN NAME		ALTERNATIVE NAME				SUB-AREA
Ⓐ Ⓥ	**Fauscoum**		*Ir: Fáschom, 'empty hollow'*				
HEIGHT METRES	COUNTY	1:50K MAP NO.	MAP GRID REF	PROMINENCE	HEIGHT RANK	MV RATING	DATE CLIMBED
792	Waterford	75	S316₈₉ 105₀₈	626m	47	7.9	

CLASSIFICATION	MOUNTAIN NAME		ALTERNATIVE NAME				SUB-AREA
Ⓥ	**Carrignagower**		*Ir: Carraig na nGabhar, 'rock of the goats'*				
HEIGHT METRES	COUNTY	1:50K MAP NO.	MAP GRID REF	PROMINENCE	HEIGHT RANK	MV RATING	DATE CLIMBED
767	Waterford	75	S311₈₄ 120₉₄	24m	61	7.6	

CLASSIFICATION	MOUNTAIN NAME		ALTERNATIVE NAME				SUB-AREA
Ⓐ Ⓥ	**Knockanaffrin**		*Ir: Cnoc an Aifrinn, 'hill of the Mass'*				
HEIGHT METRES	COUNTY	1:50K MAP NO.	MAP GRID REF	PROMINENCE	HEIGHT RANK	MV RATING	DATE CLIMBED
755	Waterford	75	S285₆₀ 152₉₀	289m	73	8.0	

CLASSIFICATION	MOUNTAIN NAME		ALTERNATIVE NAME				SUB-AREA
Ⓐ Ⓥ	**Coumfea**		*Ir: Com Fia, 'hollow of the deer'*				
HEIGHT METRES	COUNTY	1:50K MAP NO.	MAP GRID REF	PROMINENCE	HEIGHT RANK	MV RATING	DATE CLIMBED
744	Waterford	75	S295₃₀ 097₅₆	69m	80	7.6	

CLASSIFICATION	MOUNTAIN NAME		ALTERNATIVE NAME				SUB-AREA
Ⓥ	**Coumfea N Top**		*Ir: Com Fia, 'hollow of the deer'*				
HEIGHT METRES	COUNTY	1:50K MAP NO.	MAP GRID REF	PROMINENCE	HEIGHT RANK	MV RATING	DATE CLIMBED
730	Waterford	75	S295₈₁ 107₁₇	25m	87	8.3	

CLASSIFICATION	MOUNTAIN NAME		ALTERNATIVE NAME				SUB-AREA
Ⓐ Ⓥ	**Seefin**		*Ir: Mullach Suí Finn, 'summit of Fionn's seat'*				Monavullagh Mtns
HEIGHT METRES	COUNTY	1:50K MAP NO.	MAP GRID REF	PROMINENCE	HEIGHT RANK	MV RATING	DATE CLIMBED
726	Waterford	75	S274₂₀ 068₂₅	71m	89	7.4	

CLASSIFICATION	MOUNTAIN NAME		ALTERNATIVE NAME				SUB-AREA
Ⓥ	**Coumfea W Top**		*Ir: Com Fia, 'hollow of the deer'*				
HEIGHT METRES	COUNTY	1:50K MAP NO.	MAP GRID REF	PROMINENCE	HEIGHT RANK	MV RATING	DATE CLIMBED
711	Waterford	75	S281₁₂ 094₈₇	16m	101	8.3	

CLASSIFICATION	MOUNTAIN NAME		ALTERNATIVE NAME				SUB-AREA
Ⓐ	**Knocksheegowna**		*Ir: Cnoc Sí Ghamhna, 'hill of the calf's fairy mound'*				

HEIGHT METRES	COUNTY	1:50K MAP NO.	MAP GRID REF	PROMINENCE	HEIGHT RANK	MV RATING	DATE CLIMBED
678	Waterford	75	S277₇₆ 165₃₂	53m	139	8.3	

CLASSIFICATION	MOUNTAIN NAME		ALTERNATIVE NAME				SUB-AREA
Ⓐ Ⓥ	**Coumaraglin Mtn**		*Ir: Sliabh Chom Airglinn, 'mtn of Coumaraglin'*				Monavullagh Mtns

HEIGHT METRES	COUNTY	1:50K MAP NO.	MAP GRID REF	PROMINENCE	HEIGHT RANK	MV RATING	DATE CLIMBED
617	Waterford	75/82	S282₂₈ 042₄₂	102m	242	7.8	

CLASSIFICATION	MOUNTAIN NAME		ALTERNATIVE NAME				SUB-AREA
Ⓐ	**Laghtnafrankee**		*Ir: Leacht na Francaí, 'burial monument of the rat'*				

HEIGHT METRES	COUNTY	1:50K MAP NO.	MAP GRID REF	PROMINENCE	HEIGHT RANK	MV RATING	DATE CLIMBED
520	Waterford	75	S235₁₉ 181₅₁	126m	403	6.8	

The glacial amphitheatre of Coumshingaun in the Comeraghs

The upper slopes of Slieve Foye bathed in winter sun.

COOLEY/GULLION

CLASSIFICATION	MOUNTAIN NAME	ALTERNATIVE NAME					SUB-AREA
Ⓐ	**Slieve Foye**	*Ir: Sliabh Feá, 'mountain of rushes'*					Cooley Mtns
HEIGHT METRES	COUNTY	1:50K MAP NO.	MAP GRID REF	PROMINENCE	HEIGHT RANK	MV RATING	DATE CLIMBED
589	Louth	29/36A	J169$_{02}$ 119$_{34}$	494m	289	8.1	

CLASSIFICATION	MOUNTAIN NAME	ALTERNATIVE NAME					SUB-AREA
Ⓐ	**Slieve Gullion**	*Ir: Sliabh gCuillinn, 'mountain of the steep slope/holly'*					Slieve Gullion
HEIGHT METRES	COUNTY	1:50K MAP NO.	MAP GRID REF	PROMINENCE	HEIGHT RANK	MV RATING	DATE CLIMBED
573	Armagh	29	J024$_{76}$ 203$_{31}$	478m	314	6.6	

CLASSIFICATION	MOUNTAIN NAME	ALTERNATIVE NAME					SUB-AREA
Ⓐ	**Clermont Carn**	*Ir: Carnán Mhaighréid Náir, 'cairn of noble Margaret'*					Cooley Mtns
HEIGHT METRES	COUNTY	1:50K MAP NO.	MAP GRID REF	PROMINENCE	HEIGHT RANK	MV RATING	DATE CLIMBED
510	Louth	29/36A	J099$_{09}$ 157$_{58}$	312m	427	5.7	

CROAGH PATRICK

CLASSIFICATION	MOUNTAIN NAME	ALTERNATIVE NAME				SUB-AREA
🅐 🆅🅻	**Croagh Patrick**	*The Reek. Ir: Cruach Phádraig, 'Patrick's stack'*				
HEIGHT METRES	**COUNTY**	**1:50K MAP NO.**	**MAP GRID REF**	**PROMINENCE**	**HEIGHT RANK**	**MV RATING**	**DATE CLIMBED**
764	Mayo	30	L905₈₅ 801₉₇ 639m		64	6.9

CLASSIFICATION	MOUNTAIN NAME	ALTERNATIVE NAME				SUB-AREA
🅐	**Ben Goram**	*Ir: An Bhinn Ghorm, 'the blue peak'*				
HEIGHT METRES	**COUNTY**	**1:50K MAP NO.**	**MAP GRID REF**	**PROMINENCE**	**HEIGHT RANK**	**MV RATING**	**DATE CLIMBED**
559	Mayo	30	L887₇₂ 800₂₃ 74m		338	7.6

CLASSIFICATION	MOUNTAIN NAME	ALTERNATIVE NAME				SUB-AREA
🅐	**Croagh Patrick Far E Top**	*The Reek. Ir: Cruach Phádraig, 'Patrick's stack'*				
HEIGHT METRES	**COUNTY**	**1:50K MAP NO.**	**MAP GRID REF**	**PROMINENCE**	**HEIGHT RANK**	**MV RATING**	**DATE CLIMBED**
500	Mayo	31	L929₃₄ 804₅₁ 74m		452	7.0

Croagh Patrick and the East Top from the summit of Croagh Patrick Far East Top

DARTRY MOUNTAINS

CLASSIFICATION	MOUNTAIN NAME	ALTERNATIVE NAME				SUB-AREA
Ⓐ ⓋⓁ	**Truskmore**	*Ir: Trosc Mór, 'big [obscure element]'*				
HEIGHT METRES	COUNTY	1:50K MAP NO.	MAP GRID REF	PROMINENCE	HEIGHT RANK	MV RATING	DATE CLIMBED
647	Sligo	16	G758₉₉ 473₄₈	560m	195	6.9	

CLASSIFICATION	MOUNTAIN NAME	ALTERNATIVE NAME				SUB-AREA
Ⓐ ⓋⓁ	**Tievebaun**	*Ir: Taobh Bán, 'grassy slope'*				
HEIGHT METRES	COUNTY	1:50K MAP NO.	MAP GRID REF	PROMINENCE	HEIGHT RANK	MV RATING	DATE CLIMBED
611	Leitrim	16	G768₄₄ 498₉₅	106m	246	7.4	

CLASSIFICATION	MOUNTAIN NAME	ALTERNATIVE NAME				SUB-AREA
Ⓐ	**Slievemore**					
HEIGHT METRES	COUNTY	1:50K MAP NO.	MAP GRID REF	PROMINENCE	HEIGHT RANK	MV RATING	DATE CLIMBED
597	Sligo	16	G727₇₄ 463₆₃	212m	273	7.5	

CLASSIFICATION	MOUNTAIN NAME	ALTERNATIVE NAME				SUB-AREA
Ⓐ	**Benbulbin**	*Ir: Binn Ghulbain, 'Gulban's peak' or 'jaw-shaped peak'*				
HEIGHT METRES	COUNTY	1:50K MAP NO.	MAP GRID REF	PROMINENCE	HEIGHT RANK	MV RATING	DATE CLIMBED
526	Sligo	16	G692₂₆ 463₅₃	61m	394	8.4	

Benbulbin's crenellated escarpment

Crockaun's south side with distinctive cliff and scree slope

The distinctive wave-like profile of Benwiskin viewed from near Ballaghnatrillick Bridge

CLASSIFICATION	MOUNTAIN NAME		ALTERNATIVE NAME			SUB-AREA	
Ⓐ	**Arroo Mtn**		*Ir: Sliabh Aradh, 'mountain of [obscure element]'*				
HEIGHT METRES	COUNTY	1:50K MAP NO.	MAP GRID REF	PROMINENCE	HEIGHT RANK	MV RATING	DATE CLIMBED
523	Leitrim	16	G833₀₃ 520₆₀	436m	399	8.7	

CLASSIFICATION	MOUNTAIN NAME		ALTERNATIVE NAME			SUB-AREA	
Ⓐ	**Benwiskin**						
HEIGHT METRES	COUNTY	1:50K MAP NO.	MAP GRID REF	PROMINENCE	HEIGHT RANK	MV RATING	DATE CLIMBED
514	Sligo	16	G723₄₇ 491₁₆	39m	418	8.5	

DINGLE WEST

CLASSIFICATION	MOUNTAIN NAME		ALTERNATIVE NAME				SUB-AREA
Ⓐ	**Mount Eagle**		*Ir: Sliabh an Iolair, 'mountain of the eagle'*				

HEIGHT METRES	COUNTY	1:50K MAP NO.	MAP GRID REF	PROMINENCE	HEIGHT RANK	MV RATING	DATE CLIMBED
516	Kerry	70	V334₆₇ 989₄₉	461m	412	7.3	

From Mount Eagle across Blasket Sound to the Great Blasket Island

DONEGAL NORTH-WEST

CLASSIFICATION	MOUNTAIN NAME		ALTERNATIVE NAME				SUB-AREA
Ⓐ ⓋⓁ	**Errigal**		*Ir: An Earagail, poss. 'oratory'*				Derryveagh Mtns

HEIGHT METRES	COUNTY	1:50K MAP NO.	MAP GRID REF	PROMINENCE	HEIGHT RANK	MV RATING	DATE CLIMBED
751	Donegal	1	B928₂₆ 207₇₈	688m	75	7.9	

CLASSIFICATION	MOUNTAIN NAME		ALTERNATIVE NAME				SUB-AREA
Ⓐ ⓋⓁ	**Slieve Snaght**		*Ir: Sliabh Sneachta, 'mountain of snow'*				Derryveagh Mtns

HEIGHT METRES	COUNTY	1:50K MAP NO.	MAP GRID REF	PROMINENCE	HEIGHT RANK	MV RATING	DATE CLIMBED
678	Donegal	1	B923₅₉ 148₁₂	403m	138	9.1	

CLASSIFICATION	MOUNTAIN NAME		ALTERNATIVE NAME				SUB-AREA
Ⓐ ⓋⓁ	**Muckish**		*Ir: An Mhucais, 'the pig back/ridge'*				Derryveagh Mtns

HEIGHT METRES	COUNTY	1:50K MAP NO.	MAP GRID REF	PROMINENCE	HEIGHT RANK	MV RATING	DATE CLIMBED
667.1*	Donegal	2	C004₄₈ 287₀₉	523m	158	8.3	

CLASSIFICATION	MOUNTAIN NAME	ALTERNATIVE NAME				SUB-AREA
A VL	**Dooish**	*Ir: An Dubhais, 'the black ridge'*				Derryveagh Mtns
HEIGHT METRES	COUNTY	1:50K MAP NO.	MAP GRID REF	PROMINENCE	HEIGHT RANK	MV RATING	DATE CLIMBED
652	Donegal	6	B982₂₁ 210₃₇	377m	182	8.8	

CLASSIFICATION	MOUNTAIN NAME	ALTERNATIVE NAME				SUB-AREA
A VL	**Aghla Beg (South)**	*Ir: An Eachla Bheag, poss. 'little lookout point/prospect'*				Derryveagh Mtns
HEIGHT METRES	COUNTY	1:50K MAP NO.	MAP GRID REF	PROMINENCE	HEIGHT RANK	MV RATING	DATE CLIMBED
603	Donegal	2	B965₈₉ 246₆₅	368m	259	8.2	

CLASSIFICATION	MOUNTAIN NAME	ALTERNATIVE NAME				SUB-AREA
A	**Drumnalifferny Mtn**	*Ir: Sliabh Dhroim na Luifearnaí, 'mtn of Drumnalifferny'*				Derryveagh Mtns
HEIGHT METRES	COUNTY	1:50K MAP NO.	MAP GRID REF	PROMINENCE	HEIGHT RANK	MV RATING	DATE CLIMBED
596	Donegal	1	B933₁₉ 156₂₇	101m	274	8.8	

CLASSIFICATION	MOUNTAIN NAME	ALTERNATIVE NAME				SUB-AREA
A	**Aghla More**	*Ir: An Eachla Mhór, poss. 'great lookout point/prospect'*				Derryveagh Mtns
HEIGHT METRES	COUNTY	1:50K MAP NO.	MAP GRID REF	PROMINENCE	HEIGHT RANK	MV RATING	DATE CLIMBED
584	Donegal	1	B949₇₆ 239₃₄	137m	297	9.4	

Mackoght (right), Altan Lough and beyond the Aghlas from the slopes of Errigal

The summit ridge of Errigal

CLASSIFICATION	MOUNTAIN NAME		ALTERNATIVE NAME				SUB-AREA
Ⓐ	**Bingorms**		*Ir: na Beanna Gorma, 'the blue peaks'*				Derryveagh Mtns
HEIGHT METRES	**COUNTY**	**1:50K MAP NO.**	**MAP GRID REF**	**PROMINENCE**	**HEIGHT RANK**	**MV RATING**	**DATE CLIMBED**
578	Donegal	1	B933₉₈ 143₄₁	33m	305	8.3	

CLASSIFICATION	MOUNTAIN NAME		ALTERNATIVE NAME				SUB-AREA
Ⓐ	**Aghla Beg**		*Ir: An Eachla Bheag, poss. 'little lookout point/prospect'*				Derryveagh Mtns
HEIGHT METRES	**COUNTY**	**1:50K MAP NO.**	**MAP GRID REF**	**PROMINENCE**	**HEIGHT RANK**	**MV RATING**	**DATE CLIMBED**
564	Donegal	2	B961₅₄ 253₀₀	49m	329	8.3	

CLASSIFICATION	MOUNTAIN NAME		ALTERNATIVE NAME				SUB-AREA
Ⓐ	**Mackoght**		*Ir: Mac Uchta, 'son of the mountain-breast'*				Derryveagh Mtns
HEIGHT METRES	**COUNTY**	**1:50K MAP NO.**	**MAP GRID REF**	**PROMINENCE**	**HEIGHT RANK**	**MV RATING**	**DATE CLIMBED**
555	Donegal	1	B940₁₈ 214₇₄	150m	342	8.2	

CLASSIFICATION	MOUNTAIN NAME		ALTERNATIVE NAME				SUB-AREA
Ⓐ	**Dooish SE Top**						Derryveagh Mtns
HEIGHT METRES	**COUNTY**	**1:50K MAP NO.**	**MAP GRID REF**	**PROMINENCE**	**HEIGHT RANK**	**MV RATING**	**DATE CLIMBED**
555	Donegal	6	B989₁₇ 206₃₇	40m	343	6.9	

View from the trig pillar to Muckish's summit cairn. In the distance, a rainbow over Bloody Foreland

CLASSIFICATION	MOUNTAIN NAME		ALTERNATIVE NAME				SUB-AREA
Ⓐ	**Moylenanav**		*Ir: Maol na nDamh, 'bald hill of the oxen/stags'*				Glendowan Mtns
HEIGHT METRES	COUNTY	1:50K MAP NO.	MAP GRID REF	PROMINENCE	HEIGHT RANK	MV RATING	DATE CLIMBED
539	Donegal	1	B955₈₇ 133₁₁	294m	369	8.3	

CLASSIFICATION	MOUNTAIN NAME		ALTERNATIVE NAME				SUB-AREA
Ⓐ	**Crockfadda**		*Ir: An Cnoc Fada, 'the long hill'*				Derryveagh Mtns
HEIGHT METRES	COUNTY	1:50K MAP NO.	MAP GRID REF	PROMINENCE	HEIGHT RANK	MV RATING	DATE CLIMBED
529	Donegal	1	B909₉₄ 136₅₆	80m	388	7.9	

CLASSIFICATION	MOUNTAIN NAME		ALTERNATIVE NAME				SUB-AREA
Ⓐ	**Crocknafarragh**		*Ir: Cnoc na bhFaircheach, 'hill of the [?]'*				Derryveagh Mtns
HEIGHT METRES	COUNTY	1:50K MAP NO.	MAP GRID REF	PROMINENCE	HEIGHT RANK	MV RATING	DATE CLIMBED
517	Donegal	1	B878₀₉ 167₅₂	172m	410	7.1	

CLASSIFICATION	MOUNTAIN NAME		ALTERNATIVE NAME				SUB-AREA
Ⓐ	**Crockfadda NE Top**		*Ir: An Cnoc Fada, 'the long hill'*				Derryveagh Mtns
HEIGHT METRES	COUNTY	1:50K MAP NO.	MAP GRID REF	PROMINENCE	HEIGHT RANK	MV RATING	DATE CLIMBED
502	Donegal	1	B915₈₅ 144₀₃	37m	443	8.1	

CLASSIFICATION	MOUNTAIN NAME		ALTERNATIVE NAME				SUB-AREA
Ⓐ	**Saggartnadooish**		*Ir: Sagart na Dubhaise, 'chaplain/attendant of Dooish'*				Derryveagh Mtns
HEIGHT METRES	COUNTY	1:50K MAP NO.	MAP GRID REF	PROMINENCE	HEIGHT RANK	MV RATING	DATE CLIMBED
501	Donegal	6	B991₂₂ 216₈₂	56m	449	8.2	

DONEGAL SOUTH-WEST

CLASSIFICATION	MOUNTAIN NAME	ALTERNATIVE NAME				SUB-AREA
Ⓐ	**Slieve League**	*Ir: Sliabh Liag, 'mountain of the flagstones'*				

HEIGHT METRES	COUNTY	1:50K MAP NO.	MAP GRID REF	PROMINENCE	HEIGHT RANK	MV RATING	DATE CLIMBED
595	Donegal	10	G544₁₄ 783₅₉	470m	276	8.0	

CLASSIFICATION	MOUNTAIN NAME	ALTERNATIVE NAME				SUB-AREA
Ⓐ	**Slievetooey**	*Ir: Sliabh Tuaidh, 'northern mountain'*				

HEIGHT METRES	COUNTY	1:50K MAP NO.	MAP GRID REF	PROMINENCE	HEIGHT RANK	MV RATING	DATE CLIMBED
511	Donegal	10	G628₇₈ 899₃₉	376m	423	9.3	

CLASSIFICATION	MOUNTAIN NAME	ALTERNATIVE NAME				SUB-AREA
Ⓐ	**Common Mtn**	*Ir: Sliabh Chamáin, poss. 'mountain of the crooked place'*				

HEIGHT METRES	COUNTY	1:50K MAP NO.	MAP GRID REF	PROMINENCE	HEIGHT RANK	MV RATING	DATE CLIMBED
501	Donegal	10	G709₁₆ 859₄₁	316m	448	7.1	

Crockrawer, a 400m top on the way to cloud-covered Slieve League

CLASSIFICATION	MOUNTAIN NAME	ALTERNATIVE NAME				SUB-AREA
Ⓐ Ⓥ	**Lugnaquillia**	*Ir: Log na Coille, 'hollow of the wood'*				Wicklow Mtns
HEIGHT METRES	**COUNTY**	**1:50K MAP NO.**	**MAP GRID REF**	**PROMINENCE**	**HEIGHT RANK**	**MV RATING**	**DATE CLIMBED**
925	Wicklow	56	T032₁₇ 917₅₆ 905m	13	7.3	

CLASSIFICATION	MOUNTAIN NAME	ALTERNATIVE NAME				SUB-AREA
Ⓐ Ⓥ	**Mullaghcleevaun**	*Ir: Mullach Cliabháin, 'summit of the cradle/basket'*				Wicklow Mtns
HEIGHT METRES	**COUNTY**	**1:50K MAP NO.**	**MAP GRID REF**	**PROMINENCE**	**HEIGHT RANK**	**MV RATING**	**DATE CLIMBED**
849	Wicklow	56	O067₆₃ 070₄₉ 374m	20	7.4	

CLASSIFICATION	MOUNTAIN NAME	ALTERNATIVE NAME				SUB-AREA
Ⓐ Ⓥ	**Tonelagee**	*Ir: Tóin le Gaoith, 'backside to the wind'*				Wicklow Mtns
HEIGHT METRES	**COUNTY**	**1:50K MAP NO.**	**MAP GRID REF**	**PROMINENCE**	**HEIGHT RANK**	**MV RATING**	**DATE CLIMBED**
817	Wicklow	56	O085₀₃ 015₈₉ 202m	32	8.1	

CLASSIFICATION	MOUNTAIN NAME	ALTERNATIVE NAME				SUB-AREA
Ⓥ	**Cloghernagh**	*Ir: Clocharnach, 'stony place'*				Wicklow Mtns
HEIGHT METRES	**COUNTY**	**1:50K MAP NO.**	**MAP GRID REF**	**PROMINENCE**	**HEIGHT RANK**	**MV RATING**	**DATE CLIMBED**
800	Wicklow	56	T058₂₁ 918₇₉ 15m	39	6.7	

CLASSIFICATION	MOUNTAIN NAME	ALTERNATIVE NAME				SUB-AREA
Ⓐ Ⓥ	**Corrigasleggaun**	*Ir: Carraig (n)a Sliogán, 'rock of the shells or flat stones'*				Wicklow Mtns
HEIGHT METRES	**COUNTY**	**1:50K MAP NO.**	**MAP GRID REF**	**PROMINENCE**	**HEIGHT RANK**	**MV RATING**	**DATE CLIMBED**
794	Wicklow	56	T047₈₂ 910₉₃ 49m	45	6.5	

CLASSIFICATION	MOUNTAIN NAME	ALTERNATIVE NAME				SUB-AREA
Ⓐ Ⓥ	**Mullaghcleevaun E Top**	*Ir: Mullach Cliabháin, 'summit of the cradle/basket'*				Wicklow Mtns
HEIGHT METRES	**COUNTY**	**1:50K MAP NO.**	**MAP GRID REF**	**PROMINENCE**	**HEIGHT RANK**	**MV RATING**	**DATE CLIMBED**
790	Wicklow	56	O082₃₇ 066₉₅ 45m	51	7.8	

CLASSIFICATION	MOUNTAIN NAME	ALTERNATIVE NAME				SUB-AREA
Ⓐ Ⓥ	**Slievemaan**	*Ir: Sliabh Meáin, 'middle mountain'*				Wicklow Mtns
HEIGHT METRES	**COUNTY**	**1:50K MAP NO.**	**MAP GRID REF**	**PROMINENCE**	**HEIGHT RANK**	**MV RATING**	**DATE CLIMBED**
759	Wicklow	56	T017₅₆ 908₁₉ 54m	69	6.1	

CLASSIFICATION	MOUNTAIN NAME	ALTERNATIVE NAME				SUB-AREA
Ⓐ Ⓥ	**Camenabologue**	*Ir: Céim na mBulóg, 'step/pass of the bullocks'*				Wicklow Mtns
HEIGHT METRES	**COUNTY**	**1:50K MAP NO.**	**MAP GRID REF**	**PROMINENCE**	**HEIGHT RANK**	**MV RATING**	**DATE CLIMBED**
758	Wicklow	56	T023₂₁ 959₉₂ 133m	70	6.7	

CLASSIFICATION	MOUNTAIN NAME	ALTERNATIVE NAME				SUB-AREA
Ⓐ Ⓥ	**Kippure**	*Ir: Cipiúr, origin obscure*				Dublin Mtns
HEIGHT METRES	**COUNTY**	**1:50K MAP NO.**	**MAP GRID REF**	**PROMINENCE**	**HEIGHT RANK**	**MV RATING**	**DATE CLIMBED**
757	Dublin/Wicklow	56	O115₈₂ 154₅₅ 262m	72	5.7	

CLASSIFICATION	MOUNTAIN NAME	ALTERNATIVE NAME		SUB-AREA
Ⓐ ⓥ	**Conavalla**	*Ir: Ceann an Bhealaigh, 'head of the road/pass'*		Wicklow Mtns

HEIGHT METRES	COUNTY	1:50K MAP NO.	MAP GRID REF	PROMINENCE	HEIGHT RANK	MV RATING	DATE CLIMBED
734	Wicklow	56	T039₆₈ 971₅₈	109m	85	7.0	

CLASSIFICATION	MOUNTAIN NAME	ALTERNATIVE NAME		SUB-AREA
Ⓐ ⓥ	**Djouce**	*Ir: Dioghais, 'fortified height'*		Wicklow Mtns

HEIGHT METRES	COUNTY	1:50K MAP NO.	MAP GRID REF	PROMINENCE	HEIGHT RANK	MV RATING	DATE CLIMBED
725	Wicklow	56	O178₅₈ 103₆₀	200m	90	5.7	

CLASSIFICATION	MOUNTAIN NAME	ALTERNATIVE NAME		SUB-AREA
Ⓐ ⓥ	**Seefingan**	*Ir: Suí Fingain, 'Fingan's seat'*		Dublin Mtns

HEIGHT METRES	COUNTY	1:50K MAP NO.	MAP GRID REF	PROMINENCE	HEIGHT RANK	MV RATING	DATE CLIMBED
722.9*	Dublin/Wicklow	56	O086₆₇ 169₈₀	98m	91	6.7	

CLASSIFICATION	MOUNTAIN NAME	ALTERNATIVE NAME		SUB-AREA
Ⓐ ⓥ	**Duff Hill**	*Ir: An Cnoc Dubh, 'black hill'*		Wicklow Mtns

HEIGHT METRES	COUNTY	1:50K MAP NO.	MAP GRID REF	PROMINENCE	HEIGHT RANK	MV RATING	DATE CLIMBED
720	Wicklow	56	O093₈₁ 082₅₈	65m	95	7.1	

Corrigasleggaun, viewed from near the summit of Lugnaquilla

Lugnaquilla, the highest of the Wicklow mountains, seen from the east on a glorious day in winter

CLASSIFICATION	MOUNTAIN NAME		ALTERNATIVE NAME				SUB-AREA
Ⓐ Ⓥ	**Gravale**		*Ir: Droibhéal, 'difficult passage'*				Wicklow Mtns
HEIGHT METRES	COUNTY	1:50K MAP NO.	MAP GRID REF	PROMINENCE	HEIGHT RANK	MV RATING	DATE CLIMBED
718	Wicklow	56	0104₉₀ 094₂₀	123m	96	6.9	

CLASSIFICATION	MOUNTAIN NAME		ALTERNATIVE NAME				SUB-AREA
Ⓥ	**Stoney Top**						Wicklow Mtns
HEIGHT METRES	COUNTY	1:50K MAP NO.	MAP GRID REF	PROMINENCE	HEIGHT RANK	MV RATING	DATE CLIMBED
714	Wicklow	56	0082₄₆ 027₀₂	19m	99	6.5	

CLASSIFICATION	MOUNTAIN NAME		ALTERNATIVE NAME				SUB-AREA
Ⓐ Ⓥ	**Moanbane**		*Ir: Móin Bhán, 'white bog'*				Wicklow Mtns
HEIGHT METRES	COUNTY	1:50K MAP NO.	MAP GRID REF	PROMINENCE	HEIGHT RANK	MV RATING	DATE CLIMBED
703	Wicklow	56	0033₃₃ 068₈₆	108m	106	6.6	

CLASSIFICATION	MOUNTAIN NAME		ALTERNATIVE NAME				SUB-AREA
Ⓥ	**Table Mtn**						Wicklow Mtns
HEIGHT METRES	COUNTY	1:50K MAP NO.	MAP GRID REF	PROMINENCE	HEIGHT RANK	MV RATING	DATE CLIMBED
701	Wicklow	56	T019₄₇ 973₁₅	16m	108	5.7	

CLASSIFICATION	MOUNTAIN NAME		ALTERNATIVE NAME				SUB-AREA
Ⓐ Ⓥ	**Silsean**		*Ir: Soilseán, 'place of lights'*				Wicklow Mtns
HEIGHT METRES	COUNTY	1:50K MAP NO.	MAP GRID REF	PROMINENCE	HEIGHT RANK	MV RATING	DATE CLIMBED
698	Wicklow	56	0023₁₈ 056₄₉	43m	111	6.5	

CLASSIFICATION	MOUNTAIN NAME	ALTERNATIVE NAME	SUB-AREA
(A) (VL)	**Camaderry**	*Ir: Sliabh Cham an Doire, 'bend of the oak-wood'*	Wicklow Mtns

HEIGHT METRES	COUNTY	1:50K MAP NO.	MAP GRID REF	PROMINENCE	HEIGHT RANK	MV RATING	DATE CLIMBED
698	Wicklow	56	T081$_{73}$ 980$_{81}$	71m	112	6.7	

CLASSIFICATION	MOUNTAIN NAME	ALTERNATIVE NAME	SUB-AREA
(VL)	**Benleagh**	*Ir: Binn Liath, 'grey peak'*	Wicklow Mtns

HEIGHT METRES	COUNTY	1:50K MAP NO.	MAP GRID REF	PROMINENCE	HEIGHT RANK	MV RATING	DATE CLIMBED
689	Wicklow	56	T038$_{66}$ 941$_{80}$	24m	123	7.4	

CLASSIFICATION	MOUNTAIN NAME	ALTERNATIVE NAME	SUB-AREA
(A) (VL)	**War Hill**	*Ir: Cnoc an Bhairr, 'hill of the summit'*	Wicklow Mtns

HEIGHT METRES	COUNTY	1:50K MAP NO.	MAP GRID REF	PROMINENCE	HEIGHT RANK	MV RATING	DATE CLIMBED
686	Wicklow	56	O168$_{95}$ 113$_{38}$	71m	126	5.6	

CLASSIFICATION	MOUNTAIN NAME	ALTERNATIVE NAME	SUB-AREA
(A) (VL)	**Carrigvore**	*Ir: An Charraig Mhór, 'the big rock'*	Wicklow Mtns

HEIGHT METRES	COUNTY	1:50K MAP NO.	MAP GRID REF	PROMINENCE	HEIGHT RANK	MV RATING	DATE CLIMBED
682	Wicklow	56	O122$_{70}$ 101$_{42}$	67m	130	6.6	

CLASSIFICATION	MOUNTAIN NAME	ALTERNATIVE NAME	SUB-AREA
(A) (VL)	**Tomaneena**	*Ir: Tuaim an Aonaigh, 'mound of the fair'*	Wicklow Mtns

HEIGHT METRES	COUNTY	1:50K MAP NO.	MAP GRID REF	PROMINENCE	HEIGHT RANK	MV RATING	DATE CLIMBED
681	Wicklow	56	T063$_{00}$ 982$_{00}$	54m	133	5.1	

CLASSIFICATION	MOUNTAIN NAME	ALTERNATIVE NAME	SUB-AREA
(VL)	**Tonlagee NE Top**	*Ir: Tóin le Gaoith, 'backside to the wind'*	Wicklow Mtns

HEIGHT METRES	COUNTY	1:50K MAP NO.	MAP GRID REF	PROMINENCE	HEIGHT RANK	MV RATING	DATE CLIMBED
668	Wicklow	56	O095$_{68}$ 018$_{87}$	23m	155	6.8	

CLASSIFICATION	MOUNTAIN NAME	ALTERNATIVE NAME	SUB-AREA
(A) (VL)	**Croaghanamoira**	*Ir: Cruachán Mhaigh Rath, 'little stack of Moira'*	Wicklow Mtns

HEIGHT METRES	COUNTY	1:50K MAP NO.	MAP GRID REF	PROMINENCE	HEIGHT RANK	MV RATING	DATE CLIMBED
664	Wicklow	62	T099$_{22}$ 865$_{04}$	209m	164	7.6	

CLASSIFICATION	MOUNTAIN NAME	ALTERNATIVE NAME	SUB-AREA
(A) (VL)	**Camenabologue SE Top**	*Ir: Céim na mBulóg, 'step/pass of the bullocks'*	Wicklow Mtns

HEIGHT METRES	COUNTY	1:50K MAP NO.	MAP GRID REF	PROMINENCE	HEIGHT RANK	MV RATING	DATE CLIMBED
663	Wicklow	56	T036$_{65}$ 953$_{83}$	38m	167	6.0	

CLASSIFICATION	MOUNTAIN NAME	ALTERNATIVE NAME	SUB-AREA
(A) (VL)	**Mullacor**	*Ir: Mullach Mór, 'big summit'*	Wicklow Mtns

HEIGHT METRES	COUNTY	1:50K MAP NO.	MAP GRID REF	PROMINENCE	HEIGHT RANK	MV RATING	DATE CLIMBED
657	Wicklow	56	T092$_{71}$ 939$_{13}$	102m	173	6.3	

CLASSIFICATION	MOUNTAIN NAME	ALTERNATIVE NAME		SUB-AREA
Ⓐ ⓋⓁ	**Keadeen Mtn**	*Ir: Céidín, 'flat-topped hill'*		Wicklow Mtns

HEIGHT METRES	COUNTY	1:50K MAP NO.	MAP GRID REF	PROMINENCE	HEIGHT RANK	MV RATING	DATE CLIMBED
653	Wicklow	62	S953$_{95}$ 897$_{64}$	334m	181	8.1	

CLASSIFICATION	MOUNTAIN NAME	ALTERNATIVE NAME		SUB-AREA
ⓋⓁ	**Ballineddan Mtn**	*Ir: Sliabh Bhuaile an Fheadáin, 'mtn of Ballineddan'*		Wicklow Mtns

HEIGHT METRES	COUNTY	1:50K MAP NO.	MAP GRID REF	PROMINENCE	HEIGHT RANK	MV RATING	DATE CLIMBED
652	Wicklow	56	T002$_{58}$ 907$_{88}$	27m	184	6.9	

CLASSIFICATION	MOUNTAIN NAME	ALTERNATIVE NAME		SUB-AREA
Ⓐ ⓋⓁ	**Lugduff**	*Ir: Log Dubh, 'black hollow'*		Wicklow Mtns

HEIGHT METRES	COUNTY	1:50K MAP NO.	MAP GRID REF	PROMINENCE	HEIGHT RANK	MV RATING	DATE CLIMBED
652	Wicklow	56	T072$_{20}$ 953$_{61}$	97m	185	6.4	

CLASSIFICATION	MOUNTAIN NAME	ALTERNATIVE NAME		SUB-AREA
Ⓐ ⓋⓁ	**Seahan**	*Ir: Suíochán, 'seat'*		Dublin Mtns

HEIGHT METRES	COUNTY	1:50K MAP NO.	MAP GRID REF	PROMINENCE	HEIGHT RANK	MV RATING	DATE CLIMBED
647.3*	Dublin	56	O008$_{19}$ 196$_{96}$	94m	194	6.0	

CLASSIFICATION	MOUNTAIN NAME	ALTERNATIVE NAME		SUB-AREA
Ⓐ ⓋⓁ	**Tonduff**	*Ir: Tóin Dubh, 'black bottom'*		Wicklow Mtns

HEIGHT METRES	COUNTY	1:50K MAP NO.	MAP GRID REF	PROMINENCE	HEIGHT RANK	MV RATING	DATE CLIMBED
642	Wicklow	56	O159$_{44}$ 136$_{85}$	117m	200	5.7	

CLASSIFICATION	MOUNTAIN NAME	ALTERNATIVE NAME		SUB-AREA
Ⓐ ⓋⓁ	**Scarr**	*Ir: Sceir or Scor, 'sharp rock'*		Wicklow Mtns

HEIGHT METRES	COUNTY	1:50K MAP NO.	MAP GRID REF	PROMINENCE	HEIGHT RANK	MV RATING	DATE CLIMBED
641	Wicklow	56	O132$_{69}$ 018$_{29}$	231m	204	6.8	

CLASSIFICATION	MOUNTAIN NAME	ALTERNATIVE NAME		SUB-AREA
ⓋⓁ	**Lugduff SE Top**	*Ir: Log Dubh, 'black hollow'*		Wicklow Mtns

HEIGHT METRES	COUNTY	1:50K MAP NO.	MAP GRID REF	PROMINENCE	HEIGHT RANK	MV RATING	DATE CLIMBED
637	Wicklow	56	T080$_{70}$ 949$_{24}$	22m	213	6.0	

CLASSIFICATION	MOUNTAIN NAME	ALTERNATIVE NAME		SUB-AREA
Ⓐ ⓋⓁ	**Lobawn**	*Ir: Lúbán, 'little bend'*		Wicklow Mtns

HEIGHT METRES	COUNTY	1:50K MAP NO.	MAP GRID REF	PROMINENCE	HEIGHT RANK	MV RATING	DATE CLIMBED
636	Wicklow	56	S977$_{81}$ 978$_{07}$	111m	216	5.3	

CLASSIFICATION	MOUNTAIN NAME	ALTERNATIVE NAME		SUB-AREA
ⓋⓁ	**Seefin**	*Ir: Suí Finn, 'Fionn's seat'*		Dublin Mtns

HEIGHT METRES	COUNTY	1:50K MAP NO.	MAP GRID REF	PROMINENCE	HEIGHT RANK	MV RATING	DATE CLIMBED
620.6*	Wicklow	56	O073$_{97}$ 162$_{51}$	22m	235	6.7	

CLASSIFICATION	MOUNTAIN NAME	ALTERNATIVE NAME		SUB-AREA
Ⓥ	**Corrig Mtn**	*Ir: An Charraig, 'rock'*		Dublin Mtns

HEIGHT METRES	COUNTY	1:50K MAP NO.	MAP GRID REF	PROMINENCE	HEIGHT RANK	MV RATING	DATE CLIMBED
617.1*	Dublin/Wicklow	56	0090₃₈ 1937₀	28m	241	4.8	

CLASSIFICATION	MOUNTAIN NAME	ALTERNATIVE NAME		SUB-AREA
Ⓐ Ⓥ	**Croghan Kinsella**	*Ir: Cruachán, 'little stack'*		Wicklow Mtns

HEIGHT METRES	COUNTY	1:50K MAP NO.	MAP GRID REF	PROMINENCE	HEIGHT RANK	MV RATING	DATE CLIMBED
606	Wexford/Wicklow	62	T130₉₆ 728₈₅	541m	254	6.6	

Heading from Tonelagee to Stoney Top. Mullaghcleevaun is in the background

Carrigvore and Gravale in winter

49

CLASSIFICATION | MOUNTAIN NAME | ALTERNATIVE NAME | SUB-AREA

(A) (Vl) Black Hill — Wicklow Mtns

HEIGHT METRES	COUNTY	1:50K MAP NO.	MAP GRID REF	PROMINENCE	HEIGHT RANK	MV RATING	DATE CLIMBED
602.2*	Wicklow	56	0041_{35} 090_{34}	67m	263	5.2	

CLASSIFICATION | MOUNTAIN NAME | ALTERNATIVE NAME | SUB-AREA

(A) Sorrel Hill — Wicklow Mtns

HEIGHT METRES	COUNTY	1:50K MAP NO.	MAP GRID REF	PROMINENCE	HEIGHT RANK	MV RATING	DATE CLIMBED
599.5*	Wicklow	56	0042_{21} 118_{87}	154m	271	6.0	

CLASSIFICATION | MOUNTAIN NAME | ALTERNATIVE NAME | SUB-AREA

(A) Luggala — *Ir: Log an Lá, 'hollow of the [obscure element]'* — Wicklow Mtns

HEIGHT METRES	COUNTY	1:50K MAP NO.	MAP GRID REF	PROMINENCE	HEIGHT RANK	MV RATING	DATE CLIMBED
595	Wicklow	56	0150_{13} 074_{03}	110m	277	6.3	

CLASSIFICATION | MOUNTAIN NAME | ALTERNATIVE NAME | SUB-AREA

(A) Glendoo Mtn — *Ir: Log na hEala, 'hollow of the swan'* — Dublin Mtns

HEIGHT METRES	COUNTY	1:50K MAP NO.	MAP GRID REF	PROMINENCE	HEIGHT RANK	MV RATING	DATE CLIMBED
586	Dublin/Wicklow	50	0141_{52} 204_{13}	109m	294	5.0	

CLASSIFICATION | MOUNTAIN NAME | ALTERNATIVE NAME | SUB-AREA

(A) Carrigshouk — Wicklow Mtns

HEIGHT METRES	COUNTY	1:50K MAP NO.	MAP GRID REF	PROMINENCE	HEIGHT RANK	MV RATING	DATE CLIMBED
572.5*	Wicklow	56	0097_{91} 051_{64}	31m	315	6.1	

CLASSIFICATION | MOUNTAIN NAME | ALTERNATIVE NAME | SUB-AREA

(A) Maulin — *Ir: Málainn, possibly 'high or sloping ground'* — Wicklow Mtns

HEIGHT METRES	COUNTY	1:50K MAP NO.	MAP GRID REF	PROMINENCE	HEIGHT RANK	MV RATING	DATE CLIMBED
570	Wicklow	56	0184_{37} 131_{03}	70m	320	6.1	

CLASSIFICATION | MOUNTAIN NAME | ALTERNATIVE NAME | SUB-AREA

(A) Brockagh Mtn — *Ir: Sliabh na Brocaí, 'mtn of Brocach or place of badgers'* — Wicklow Mtns

HEIGHT METRES	COUNTY	1:50K MAP NO.	MAP GRID REF	PROMINENCE	HEIGHT RANK	MV RATING	DATE CLIMBED
557	Wicklow	56	T108_{58} 990_{57}	32m	339	5.8	

CLASSIFICATION | MOUNTAIN NAME | ALTERNATIVE NAME | SUB-AREA

(A) Knocknagun — *Ir: Cnoc na gCon, 'hill of the dogs'* — Dublin Mtns

HEIGHT METRES	COUNTY	1:50K MAP NO.	MAP GRID REF	PROMINENCE	HEIGHT RANK	MV RATING	DATE CLIMBED
555	Dublin/Wicklow	56	0163_{67} 185_{53}	63m	344	6.0	

CLASSIFICATION | MOUNTAIN NAME | ALTERNATIVE NAME | SUB-AREA

(A) Prince William's Seat — Dublin Mtns

HEIGHT METRES	COUNTY	1:50K MAP NO.	MAP GRID REF	PROMINENCE	HEIGHT RANK	MV RATING	DATE CLIMBED
555	Dublin/Wicklow	56	0176_{88} 182_{78}	63m	345	5.2	

The Kilbride Circuit: Seahan, Corrig and Seefingan viewed from Seefin

Trig pillar on Croaghanmoira summit

CLASSIFICATION	MOUNTAIN NAME	ALTERNATIVE NAME	SUB-AREA
A	**Slieve Maan**	*Ir: Sliabh Meáin, 'middle mountain'*	Wicklow Mtns

HEIGHT METRES	COUNTY	1:50K MAP NO.	MAP GRID REF	PROMINENCE	HEIGHT RANK	MV RATING	DATE CLIMBED
550	Wicklow	62	T083$_{95}$ 887$_{33}$	95m	352	3.8	

CLASSIFICATION	MOUNTAIN NAME	ALTERNATIVE NAME	SUB-AREA
A	**Church Mtn**	*Ir: Sliabh gCod, 'mtn of the [obscure element]'*	Wicklow Mtns

HEIGHT METRES	COUNTY	1:50K MAP NO.	MAP GRID REF	PROMINENCE	HEIGHT RANK	MV RATING	DATE CLIMBED
544	Wicklow	56	N948$_{77}$ 012$_{61}$	129m	359	6.8	

CLASSIFICATION	MOUNTAIN NAME	ALTERNATIVE NAME	SUB-AREA
A	**Ballycurragh Hill**	*Rathhinder*	Wicklow Mtns

HEIGHT METRES	COUNTY	1:50K MAP NO.	MAP GRID REF	PROMINENCE	HEIGHT RANK	MV RATING	DATE CLIMBED
536	Wicklow	62	T057$_{00}$ 823$_{00}$	221m	373	4.3	

CLASSIFICATION	MOUNTAIN NAME	ALTERNATIVE NAME	SUB-AREA
A	**Two Rock Mtn**	*Ir: Sliab Lecga, 'mountain of flagstones'*	Dublin Mtns

HEIGHT METRES	COUNTY	1:50K MAP NO.	MAP GRID REF	PROMINENCE	HEIGHT RANK	MV RATING	DATE CLIMBED
536	Dublin	50	O172$_{18}$ 223$_{80}$	171m	374	5.0	

CLASSIFICATION	MOUNTAIN NAME	ALTERNATIVE NAME	SUB-AREA
A	**Knocknacloghoge**	*Ir: Cnoc na Clochóige, 'hill of the stony land'*	Wicklow Mtns

HEIGHT METRES	COUNTY	1:50K MAP NO.	MAP GRID REF	PROMINENCE	HEIGHT RANK	MV RATING	DATE CLIMBED
534	Wicklow	56	O143$_{57}$ 054$_{42}$	129m	378	7.4	

CLASSIFICATION	MOUNTAIN NAME	ALTERNATIVE NAME	SUB-AREA
A	**Corriebracks**	*Ir: Coire Breac, 'speckled hollow'*	Wicklow Mtns

HEIGHT METRES	COUNTY	1:50K MAP NO.	MAP GRID REF	PROMINENCE	HEIGHT RANK	MV RATING	DATE CLIMBED
531	Wicklow	56	N967$_{38}$ 002$_{68}$	116m	384	5.1	

CLASSIFICATION	MOUNTAIN NAME	ALTERNATIVE NAME	SUB-AREA
A	**Ballinacor Mtn**	*Ir: Sliabh Bhaile na Corra, 'hill of Baile na Corra'*	Wicklow Mtns

HEIGHT METRES	COUNTY	1:50K MAP NO.	MAP GRID REF	PROMINENCE	HEIGHT RANK	MV RATING	DATE CLIMBED
531	Wicklow	62	T117$_{09}$ 864$_{86}$	56m	385	5.0	

CLASSIFICATION	MOUNTAIN NAME	ALTERNATIVE NAME	SUB-AREA
A	**Carrickashane Mtn**		Wicklow Mtns

HEIGHT METRES	COUNTY	1:50K MAP NO.	MAP GRID REF	PROMINENCE	HEIGHT RANK	MV RATING	DATE CLIMBED
508	Wicklow	62	T078$_{26}$ 859$_{79}$	43m	432	4.1	

CLASSIFICATION	MOUNTAIN NAME	ALTERNATIVE NAME	SUB-AREA
A	**Great Sugar Loaf**	*Ir: Ó Cualann, 'lump of Cualu'*	Wicklow Mtns

HEIGHT METRES	COUNTY	1:50K MAP NO.	MAP GRID REF	PROMINENCE	HEIGHT RANK	MV RATING	DATE CLIMBED
501	Wicklow	56	O237$_{76}$ 130$_{88}$	216m	450	5.8	

CLASSIFICATION	MOUNTAIN NAME	ALTERNATIVE NAME				SUB-AREA
Ⓐ Ⓥ	**Stumpa Dúloigh**	*Ir: Stumpa Dúloigh, 'stump of the black lake'*				
HEIGHT METRES	COUNTY	1:50K MAP NO. MAP GRID REF	PROMINENCE	HEIGHT RANK	MV RATING	DATE CLIMBED
784	Kerry	78	V787$_{00}$ 793$_{84}$ 499m	54	8.9	

CLASSIFICATION	MOUNTAIN NAME	ALTERNATIVE NAME				SUB-AREA
Ⓥ	**Stumpa Dúloigh SE Top**	*Ir: Stumpa Dúloigh, 'stump of the black lake'*				
HEIGHT METRES	COUNTY	1:50K MAP NO. MAP GRID REF	PROMINENCE	HEIGHT RANK	MV RATING	DATE CLIMBED
780	Kerry	78	V790$_{34}$ 791$_{56}$ 15m	56	8.7	

CLASSIFICATION	MOUNTAIN NAME	ALTERNATIVE NAME				SUB-AREA
Ⓐ Ⓥ	**Mullaghanattin**	*Ir: Mullach an Aitinn, 'summit of the gorse'*				
HEIGHT METRES	COUNTY	1:50K MAP NO. MAP GRID REF	PROMINENCE	HEIGHT RANK	MV RATING	DATE CLIMBED
773	Kerry	78	V738$_{72}$ 772$_{76}$ 528m	57	9.2	

CLASSIFICATION	MOUNTAIN NAME	ALTERNATIVE NAME				SUB-AREA
Ⓐ Ⓥ	**Beann**	*Ir: An Bheann Bhán, 'white peak'*				
HEIGHT METRES	COUNTY	1:50K MAP NO. MAP GRID REF	PROMINENCE	HEIGHT RANK	MV RATING	DATE CLIMBED
752	Kerry	78	V725$_{94}$ 764$_{61}$ 64m	74	8.8	

CLASSIFICATION	MOUNTAIN NAME	ALTERNATIVE NAME				SUB-AREA
Ⓐ Ⓥ	**Broaghnabinnia**	*Ir: Bruach na Binne, 'verge of the peak'*				
HEIGHT METRES	COUNTY	1:50K MAP NO. MAP GRID REF	PROMINENCE	HEIGHT RANK	MV RATING	DATE CLIMBED
745	Kerry	78	V801$_{63}$ 813$_{88}$ 290m	79	9.5	

CLASSIFICATION	MOUNTAIN NAME	ALTERNATIVE NAME				SUB-AREA
Ⓐ Ⓥ	**Beann NE Top**	*Ir: An Bheann Bhán, 'white peak'*				
HEIGHT METRES	COUNTY	1:50K MAP NO. MAP GRID REF	PROMINENCE	HEIGHT RANK	MV RATING	DATE CLIMBED
692	Kerry	78	V730$_{86}$ 771$_{02}$ 37m	117	8.3	

CLASSIFICATION	MOUNTAIN NAME	ALTERNATIVE NAME				SUB-AREA
Ⓐ Ⓥ	**Knockmoyle**	*Ir: Cnoc Maol, 'bald or round hill'*				
HEIGHT METRES	COUNTY	1:50K MAP NO. MAP GRID REF	PROMINENCE	HEIGHT RANK	MV RATING	DATE CLIMBED
684	Kerry	78/83	V665$_{14}$ 749$_{82}$ 169m	128	7.5	

CLASSIFICATION	MOUNTAIN NAME	ALTERNATIVE NAME				SUB-AREA
Ⓐ Ⓥ	**Knocknagantee**	*Ir: Cnoc na gCainte, 'hill of the conversations'*				
HEIGHT METRES	COUNTY	1:50K MAP NO. MAP GRID REF	PROMINENCE	HEIGHT RANK	MV RATING	DATE CLIMBED
676	Kerry	78/83	V667$_{98}$ 729$_{94}$ 101m	143	8.6	

CLASSIFICATION	MOUNTAIN NAME	ALTERNATIVE NAME				SUB-AREA
Ⓐ Ⓥ	**An Bheann Mhór**	*Means 'the big peak'*				
HEIGHT METRES	COUNTY	1:50K MAP NO. MAP GRID REF	PROMINENCE	HEIGHT RANK	MV RATING	DATE CLIMBED
674.7*	Kerry	83/84	V593$_{58}$ 683$_{48}$ 290m	144	8.2	

Ascending Coomura via the south-west ridge

CLASSIFICATION	MOUNTAIN NAME	ALTERNATIVE NAME					SUB-AREA
VL	**Beann na Stiocairí**	*Means 'peak of the niggardly persons'*					
HEIGHT METRES	COUNTY	1:50K MAP NO.	MAP GRID REF	PROMINENCE	HEIGHT RANK	MV RATING	DATE CLIMBED
673.1*	Kerry	83/84	V598₈₈ 682₀₇ 20m		148	8.2	

CLASSIFICATION	MOUNTAIN NAME	ALTERNATIVE NAME					SUB-AREA
A VL	**Finnararagh**	*Ir: An Corrán, 'the crescent' or 'the sickle'*					
HEIGHT METRES	COUNTY	1:50K MAP NO.	MAP GRID REF	PROMINENCE	HEIGHT RANK	MV RATING	DATE CLIMBED
667	Kerry	78	V696₇₃ 737₃₁	142m	156	9.1	

CLASSIFICATION	MOUNTAIN NAME	ALTERNATIVE NAME					SUB-AREA
A VL	**Coomura Mtn**						
HEIGHT METRES	COUNTY	1:50K MAP NO.	MAP GRID REF	PROMINENCE	HEIGHT RANK	MV RATING	DATE CLIMBED
666	Kerry	78/83	V677₂₃ 751₇₈	111m	159	9.1	

CLASSIFICATION	MOUNTAIN NAME	ALTERNATIVE NAME					SUB-AREA
A VL	**Stumpa Dúloigh SW Top**	*Ir: Stumpa Dúloigh, 'stump of the black lake'*					
HEIGHT METRES	COUNTY	1:50K MAP NO.	MAP GRID REF	PROMINENCE	HEIGHT RANK	MV RATING	DATE CLIMBED
663	Kerry	78	V778₄₅ 789₀₅	58m	165	8.9	

CLASSIFICATION	MOUNTAIN NAME		ALTERNATIVE NAME			SUB-AREA	
Ⓐ Ⓥ	**Beann SW Top**		*Ir: An Bheann Bhán, 'white peak'*				

HEIGHT METRES	COUNTY	1:50K MAP NO.	MAP GRID REF	PROMINENCE	HEIGHT RANK	MV RATING	DATE CLIMBED
657	Kerry	78	V718₆₉ 760₁₃	72m	172	8.1	

CLASSIFICATION	MOUNTAIN NAME		ALTERNATIVE NAME			SUB-AREA	
Ⓐ Ⓥ	**Coomcallee**		*Ir: Com Caillí, 'hollow of the hag'*				

HEIGHT METRES	COUNTY	1:50K MAP NO.	MAP GRID REF	PROMINENCE	HEIGHT RANK	MV RATING	DATE CLIMBED
648.9*	Kerry	83/84	V623₉₂ 677₂₀	104m	191	8.0	

CLASSIFICATION	MOUNTAIN NAME		ALTERNATIVE NAME			SUB-AREA	
Ⓐ Ⓥ	**Knocklomena**		*Ir: Cnoc an Mheannáin, 'hill of the kid (goat)'*				

HEIGHT METRES	COUNTY	1:50K MAP NO.	MAP GRID REF	PROMINENCE	HEIGHT RANK	MV RATING	DATE CLIMBED
641	Kerry	78	V797₅₀ 765₆₈	406m	202	8.6	

CLASSIFICATION	MOUNTAIN NAME		ALTERNATIVE NAME			SUB-AREA	
Ⓐ Ⓥ	**Beann S Top**		*Ir: An Bheann Bhán, 'white peak'*				

HEIGHT METRES	COUNTY	1:50K MAP NO.	MAP GRID REF	PROMINENCE	HEIGHT RANK	MV RATING	DATE CLIMBED
639	Kerry	78	V728₁₇ 755₈₁	64m	207	7.5	

CLASSIFICATION	MOUNTAIN NAME		ALTERNATIVE NAME			SUB-AREA	
Ⓐ Ⓥ	**Cnoc na gCapall**		*Ir: Cnoc na gCapall, 'hill of the horses'*				

HEIGHT METRES	COUNTY	1:50K MAP NO.	MAP GRID REF	PROMINENCE	HEIGHT RANK	MV RATING	DATE CLIMBED
639	Kerry	78	V834₀₄ 767₃₀	334m	208	8.0	

CLASSIFICATION	MOUNTAIN NAME		ALTERNATIVE NAME			SUB-AREA	
Ⓥ	**Beann Far SW Top**		*Ir: An Bheann Bhán, 'white peak'*				

HEIGHT METRES	COUNTY	1:50K MAP NO.	MAP GRID REF	PROMINENCE	HEIGHT RANK	MV RATING	DATE CLIMBED
636	Kerry	78	V713₅₇ 754₃₅	24m	215	8.3	

CLASSIFICATION	MOUNTAIN NAME		ALTERNATIVE NAME			SUB-AREA	
Ⓐ Ⓥ	**Coomnacronia**		*Ir: Com na Cróine, 'hollow of the red cow'*				

HEIGHT METRES	COUNTY	1:50K MAP NO.	MAP GRID REF	PROMINENCE	HEIGHT RANK	MV RATING	DATE CLIMBED
636	Kerry	78/83	V679₉₆ 733₄₇	71m	214	8.4	

CLASSIFICATION	MOUNTAIN NAME		ALTERNATIVE NAME			SUB-AREA	
Ⓐ Ⓥ	**Boughil**		*Ir: Buachaill Finnleithid, 'cowherd of Finlehid'*				

HEIGHT METRES	COUNTY	1:50K MAP NO.	MAP GRID REF	PROMINENCE	HEIGHT RANK	MV RATING	DATE CLIMBED
631	Kerry	78	V841₉₁ 764₉₇	86m	221	8.7	

CLASSIFICATION	MOUNTAIN NAME		ALTERNATIVE NAME			SUB-AREA	
Ⓐ	**Bascadh**		*Ir: Bascadh, 'mutilation' or 'severe wounding'*				

HEIGHT METRES	COUNTY	1:50K MAP NO.	MAP GRID REF	PROMINENCE	HEIGHT RANK	MV RATING	DATE CLIMBED
595	Kerry	78	V823₈₇ 765₈₂	110m	275	8.1	

CLASSIFICATION	MOUNTAIN NAME		ALTERNATIVE NAME				SUB-AREA
A	**Cnoc Breasail**		*Means 'hill of raddle'*				

HEIGHT METRES	COUNTY	1:50K MAP NO.	MAP GRID REF	PROMINENCE	HEIGHT RANK	MV RATING	DATE CLIMBED
591	Kerry	78/83	V653₃₅ 724₆₉ 56m		284	8.1	

CLASSIFICATION	MOUNTAIN NAME		ALTERNATIVE NAME				SUB-AREA
A	**Coomnahorna**		*Ir. Com na hEorna, 'hollow of the barley'*				

HEIGHT METRES	COUNTY	1:50K MAP NO.	MAP GRID REF	PROMINENCE	HEIGHT RANK	MV RATING	DATE CLIMBED
590	Kerry	83/84	V639₄₄ 684₄₉ 136m		285	9.3	

CLASSIFICATION	MOUNTAIN NAME		ALTERNATIVE NAME				SUB-AREA
A	**Coomcathcun**		*Ir: Com Cait Con, 'hollow of the cat and the hound'*				

HEIGHT METRES	COUNTY	1:50K MAP NO.	MAP GRID REF	PROMINENCE	HEIGHT RANK	MV RATING	DATE CLIMBED
578	Kerry	78/83	V642₆₆ 708₁₈ 123m		304	8.3	

The approach to Sallagh (*Caora Bhán*) on the western ridge

CLASSIFICATION	MOUNTAIN NAME	ALTERNATIVE NAME		SUB-AREA
(A)	**Sallagh**	*Ir: Caora Bhán, 'white sheep'*		

HEIGHT METRES	COUNTY	1:50K MAP NO.	MAP GRID REF	PROMINENCE	HEIGHT RANK	MV RATING	DATE CLIMBED
570	Kerry	78	V705$_{05}$ 746$_{98}$	32m	319	9.0	

CLASSIFICATION	MOUNTAIN NAME	ALTERNATIVE NAME		SUB-AREA
(A)	**Knockaunanattin**	*Ir: Stumpa an Aitinn, 'stump of the gorse'*		

HEIGHT METRES	COUNTY	1:50K MAP NO.	MAP GRID REF	PROMINENCE	HEIGHT RANK	MV RATING	DATE CLIMBED
569	Kerry	78	V769$_{35}$ 790$_{98}$	54m	321	8.6	

CLASSIFICATION	MOUNTAIN NAME	ALTERNATIVE NAME		SUB-AREA
(A)	**Knocknabreeda**	*Ir: An Cnoc Breac, 'the speckled hill'*		

HEIGHT METRES	COUNTY	1:50K MAP NO.	MAP GRID REF	PROMINENCE	HEIGHT RANK	MV RATING	DATE CLIMBED
569	Kerry	78	V815$_{01}$ 793$_{37}$	74m	322	7.1	

CLASSIFICATION	MOUNTAIN NAME	ALTERNATIVE NAME		SUB-AREA
(A)	**Eagles Hill**	*Ir: An Bhinn Riabhach, 'the brindled peak'*		

HEIGHT METRES	COUNTY	1:50K MAP NO.	MAP GRID REF	PROMINENCE	HEIGHT RANK	MV RATING	DATE CLIMBED
549	Kerry	83/84	V583$_{00}$ 632$_{00}$	234m	354	8.3	

CLASSIFICATION	MOUNTAIN NAME	ALTERNATIVE NAME		SUB-AREA
(A)	**Knocknacusha**	*Ir: Cnoc Osaidh, 'hill of the encampment'*		

HEIGHT METRES	COUNTY	1:50K MAP NO.	MAP GRID REF	PROMINENCE	HEIGHT RANK	MV RATING	DATE CLIMBED
547	Kerry	78/83	V675$_{42}$ 782$_{31}$	252m	356	6.9	

CLASSIFICATION	MOUNTAIN NAME	ALTERNATIVE NAME		SUB-AREA
(A)	**An Cnoc Riabhach**	*Ir: An Cnoc Riabhach, 'the grey/striped hill'*		

HEIGHT METRES	COUNTY	1:50K MAP NO.	MAP GRID REF	PROMINENCE	HEIGHT RANK	MV RATING	DATE CLIMBED
534	Kerry	78	V758$_{16}$ 759$_{86}$	79m	377	7.0	

CLASSIFICATION	MOUNTAIN NAME	ALTERNATIVE NAME		SUB-AREA
(A)	**An Bhinn Láir**	*Ir: An Bhinn Láir, 'the middle peak'*		

HEIGHT METRES	COUNTY	1:50K MAP NO.	MAP GRID REF	PROMINENCE	HEIGHT RANK	MV RATING	DATE CLIMBED
514	Kerry	78/83	V629$_{99}$ 714$_{61}$	65m	417	8.8	

CLASSIFICATION	MOUNTAIN NAME	ALTERNATIVE NAME		SUB-AREA
(A)	**Mullaghbeg**	*Ir: Mullach Bog, 'soft summit'*		

HEIGHT METRES	COUNTY	1:50K MAP NO.	MAP GRID REF	PROMINENCE	HEIGHT RANK	MV RATING	DATE CLIMBED
509	Kerry	83/84	V559$_{00}$ 637$_{00}$	64m	428	8.6	

CLASSIFICATION	MOUNTAIN NAME	ALTERNATIVE NAME		SUB-AREA
(A)	**Mothaillín**	*Ir: Mothaillín, 'little tufted hill'*		

HEIGHT METRES	COUNTY	1:50K MAP NO.	MAP GRID REF	PROMINENCE	HEIGHT RANK	MV RATING	DATE CLIMBED
506	Kerry	78	V852$_{46}$ 805$_{07}$	92m	435	7.4	

East from Temple Hill: Lyracappul and Knockaterriff Beg, with snow-capped Galtymore in the distance

GALTY MOUNTAINS

CLASSIFICATION	MOUNTAIN NAME	ALTERNATIVE NAME		SUB-AREA
Ⓐ Ⓥ	**Galtymore**	*Ir: Cnoc Mór na nGaibhlte, 'big hill of the Galtees'*		

HEIGHT METRES	COUNTY	1:50K MAP NO.	MAP GRID REF	PROMINENCE	HEIGHT RANK	MV RATING	DATE CLIMBED
917.9*	Limerick/Tipperary	74	R87₄₆ 237₈₈	898m	14	7.9	

CLASSIFICATION	MOUNTAIN NAME	ALTERNATIVE NAME		SUB-AREA
Ⓐ Ⓥ	**Lyracappul**	*Ir: Ladhar an Chapaill, 'fork/confluence of the horse'*		

HEIGHT METRES	COUNTY	1:50K MAP NO.	MAP GRID REF	PROMINENCE	HEIGHT RANK	MV RATING	DATE CLIMBED
825	Limerick	74	R845₆₂ 231₇₉	100m	29	8.9	

CLASSIFICATION	MOUNTAIN NAME	ALTERNATIVE NAME		SUB-AREA
Ⓥ	**Carrignabinnia**	*Ir: Carraig na Binne, 'rock of the peak'*		

HEIGHT METRES	COUNTY	1:50K MAP NO.	MAP GRID REF	PROMINENCE	HEIGHT RANK	MV RATING	DATE CLIMBED
822	Limerick	74	R850₀₈ 237₀₀	27m	31	7.8	

CLASSIFICATION	MOUNTAIN NAME	ALTERNATIVE NAME		SUB-AREA
Ⓐ Ⓥ	**Greenane**	*Ir: An Grianán, 'sunny spot'*		

HEIGHT METRES	COUNTY	1:50K MAP NO.	MAP GRID REF	PROMINENCE	HEIGHT RANK	MV RATING	DATE CLIMBED
802	Tipperary	74	R925₀₀ 239₂₇	157m	38	7.3	

CLASSIFICATION	MOUNTAIN NAME	ALTERNATIVE NAME		SUB-AREA
Ⓐ Ⓥ	**Galtybeg**	*Ir: Cnoc Beag na nGaibhlte, 'little hill of the Galtees'*		

HEIGHT METRES	COUNTY	1:50K MAP NO.	MAP GRID REF	PROMINENCE	HEIGHT RANK	MV RATING	DATE CLIMBED
799.2*	Tipperary	74	R889₇₈ 240₈₉	80m	40	7.4	

CLASSIFICATION	MOUNTAIN NAME		ALTERNATIVE NAME				SUB-AREA
VL	**Lough Curra Mtn**						
HEIGHT METRES	**COUNTY**	**1:50K MAP NO.**	**MAP GRID REF**	**PROMINENCE**	**HEIGHT RANK**	**MV RATING**	**DATE CLIMBED**
600.4*	Tipperary	74	R869$_{20}$ 242$_{13}$	23m	268	6.6	

CLASSIFICATION	MOUNTAIN NAME		ALTERNATIVE NAME				SUB-AREA
A	**Knockastakeen**		*Ir: Cnoc an Stáicín, 'hill of the little stack'*				
HEIGHT METRES	**COUNTY**	**1:50K MAP NO.**	**MAP GRID REF**	**PROMINENCE**	**HEIGHT RANK**	**MV RATING**	**DATE CLIMBED**
583	Tipperary	74	R915$_{21}$ 258$_{18}$	78m	298	7.7	

CLASSIFICATION	MOUNTAIN NAME		ALTERNATIVE NAME				SUB-AREA
A	**Sturrakeen**		*Ir: An Starraicín, 'pointed peak' or 'the steeple'*				
HEIGHT METRES	**COUNTY**	**1:50K MAP NO.**	**MAP GRID REF**	**PROMINENCE**	**HEIGHT RANK**	**MV RATING**	**DATE CLIMBED**
541	Tipperary	74	R972$_{79}$ 253$_{26}$	46m	367	7.1	

GLENBEIGH HORSESHOE

CLASSIFICATION	MOUNTAIN NAME		ALTERNATIVE NAME				SUB-AREA
A VL	**Coomacarrea**		*Ir: Com an Charria, 'hollow of the stag'*				
HEIGHT METRES	**COUNTY**	**1:50K MAP NO.**	**MAP GRID REF**	**PROMINENCE**	**HEIGHT RANK**	**MV RATING**	**DATE CLIMBED**
772	Kerry	78/83	V611$_{26}$ 825$_{35}$	457m	58	9.0	

CLASSIFICATION	MOUNTAIN NAME		ALTERNATIVE NAME				SUB-AREA
VL	**Teeromoyle Mtn**		*Ir: Sliabh Thír Ó mBaoill, 'mtn of Tír Ó mBaoill'*				
HEIGHT METRES	**COUNTY**	**1:50K MAP NO.**	**MAP GRID REF**	**PROMINENCE**	**HEIGHT RANK**	**MV RATING**	**DATE CLIMBED**
760	Kerry	78/83	V603$_{78}$ 832$_{88}$	25m	68	8.9	

CLASSIFICATION	MOUNTAIN NAME		ALTERNATIVE NAME				SUB-AREA
A VL	**Meenteog**		*Ir: Muing, 'boggy area with long grass'*				
HEIGHT METRES	**COUNTY**	**1:50K MAP NO.**	**MAP GRID REF**	**PROMINENCE**	**HEIGHT RANK**	**MV RATING**	**DATE CLIMBED**
715	Kerry	78/83	V638$_{01}$ 826$_{61}$	110m	98	9.2	

CLASSIFICATION	MOUNTAIN NAME		ALTERNATIVE NAME				SUB-AREA
A VL	**Colly**		*Ir: An Bheann Mhór, 'the big peak'*				
HEIGHT METRES	**COUNTY**	**1:50K MAP NO.**	**MAP GRID REF**	**PROMINENCE**	**HEIGHT RANK**	**MV RATING**	**DATE CLIMBED**
679	Kerry	78/83	V650$_{73}$ 807$_{61}$	144m	136	8.4	

CLASSIFICATION	MOUNTAIN NAME		ALTERNATIVE NAME				SUB-AREA
A VL	**Mullaghnarakill**		*Ir: Mullach na ?, 'summit of the [obscure element]'*				
HEIGHT METRES	**COUNTY**	**1:50K MAP NO.**	**MAP GRID REF**	**PROMINENCE**	**HEIGHT RANK**	**MV RATING**	**DATE CLIMBED**
665	Kerry	78/83	V600$_{86}$ 850$_{57}$	90m	160	8.6	

CLASSIFICATION	MOUNTAIN NAME		ALTERNATIVE NAME				SUB-AREA
A VL	**Beenmore**		*Ir: Binn Mhór, 'big peak'*				
HEIGHT METRES	**COUNTY**	**1:50K MAP NO.**	**MAP GRID REF**	**PROMINENCE**	**HEIGHT RANK**	**MV RATING**	**DATE CLIMBED**
660	Kerry	83	V596$_{40}$ 867$_{91}$	125m	169	9.3	

CLASSIFICATION	MOUNTAIN NAME		ALTERNATIVE NAME				SUB-AREA
Ⓐ Ⓥ	**Been Hill**		*Ir: Beann, 'peak'*				

HEIGHT METRES	COUNTY	1:50K MAP NO.	MAP GRID REF	PROMINENCE	HEIGHT RANK	MV RATING	DATE CLIMBED
651	Kerry	83	V589₄₁ 854₁₆	46m	186	8.6	

CLASSIFICATION	MOUNTAIN NAME		ALTERNATIVE NAME				SUB-AREA
Ⓐ Ⓥ	**Drung Hill**		*Ir: Cnoc Droinge, 'hill of the throng/assembly'*				

HEIGHT METRES	COUNTY	1:50K MAP NO.	MAP GRID REF	PROMINENCE	HEIGHT RANK	MV RATING	DATE CLIMBED
640	Kerry	78/83	V602₇₆ 878₀₄	35m	205	9.2	

CLASSIFICATION	MOUNTAIN NAME		ALTERNATIVE NAME				SUB-AREA
Ⓐ Ⓥ	**Macklaun**		*Ir: Mothallán, 'little tufted hill'*				

HEIGHT METRES	COUNTY	1:50K MAP NO.	MAP GRID REF	PROMINENCE	HEIGHT RANK	MV RATING	DATE CLIMBED
607	Kerry	78/83	V660₀₀ 836₈₄	52m	252	9.1	

CLASSIFICATION	MOUNTAIN NAME		ALTERNATIVE NAME				SUB-AREA
Ⓐ	**Caunoge**						

HEIGHT METRES	COUNTY	1:50K MAP NO.	MAP GRID REF	PROMINENCE	HEIGHT RANK	MV RATING	DATE CLIMBED
502	Kerry	83	V582₆₂ 799₆₉	127m	442	7.1	

Meenteog from the east **61**

The large circular cairn enclosing the trig pillar on Slieve Snacht in Inishowen

INISHOWEN

CLASSIFICATION	MOUNTAIN NAME		ALTERNATIVE NAME				SUB-AREA
Ⓐ ⓋⓁ	**Slieve Snaght**		*Ir: Sliabh Sneachta, 'mountain of snow'*				
HEIGHT METRES	COUNTY	1:50K MAP NO.	MAP GRID REF	PROMINENCE	HEIGHT RANK	MV RATING	DATE CLIMBED
615	Donegal	3	C424₀₀ 390₀₀	600m	243	8.1	

CLASSIFICATION	MOUNTAIN NAME		ALTERNATIVE NAME				SUB-AREA
Ⓐ	**Slieve Main**		*Ir: Sliabh Meáin, 'middle mountain'*				
HEIGHT METRES	COUNTY	1:50K MAP NO.	MAP GRID REF	PROMINENCE	HEIGHT RANK	MV RATING	DATE CLIMBED
514	Donegal	3	C412₈₇ 377₉₇	100m	420	7.6	

CLASSIFICATION	MOUNTAIN NAME		ALTERNATIVE NAME				SUB-AREA
Ⓐ	**Raghtin More**		*Ir. Reachtain Mhór, 'big [obscure element]'*				
HEIGHT METRES	COUNTY	1:50K MAP NO.	MAP GRID REF	PROMINENCE	HEIGHT RANK	MV RATING	DATE CLIMBED
502	Donegal	2/3	C338₉₀ 455₇₇	407m	445	8.7	

CLASSIFICATION	MOUNTAIN NAME	ALTERNATIVE NAME				SUB-AREA
Ⓐ Ⓥ	**Knocknadobar**	*Ir: Cnoc na dTobar, 'hill of the wells'*				
HEIGHT METRES	COUNTY	1:50K MAP NO. MAP GRID REF	PROMINENCE	HEIGHT RANK	MV RATING	DATE CLIMBED
690	Kerry	83 V506₄₈ 845₁₆	565m	121	8.2	

CLASSIFICATION	MOUNTAIN NAME	ALTERNATIVE NAME				SUB-AREA
Ⓐ Ⓥ	**Kells Mtn**	*Ir: Na Cealla*				
HEIGHT METRES	COUNTY	1:50K MAP NO. MAP GRID REF	PROMINENCE	HEIGHT RANK	MV RATING	DATE CLIMBED
633	Kerry	83 V528₀₆ 858₂₆	138m	218	7.9	

CLASSIFICATION	MOUNTAIN NAME	ALTERNATIVE NAME				SUB-AREA
Ⓥ	**Kells Mtn E Top**	*Ir: Na Cealla*				
HEIGHT METRES	COUNTY	1:50K MAP NO. MAP GRID REF	PROMINENCE	HEIGHT RANK	MV RATING	DATE CLIMBED
612	Kerry	83 V536₃₃ 860₃₁	27m	244	7.1	

CLASSIFICATION	MOUNTAIN NAME	ALTERNATIVE NAME				SUB-AREA
Ⓥ	**Knocknadobar N Top**	*Ir: Cnoc na dTobar, 'hill of the wells'*				
HEIGHT METRES	COUNTY	1:50K MAP NO. MAP GRID REF	PROMINENCE	HEIGHT RANK	MV RATING	DATE CLIMBED
602	Kerry	83 V500₈₈ 854₁₃	17m	260	7.9	

Kells Mountain viewed across the bay from the Dingle Peninsula

CLASSIFICATION	MOUNTAIN NAME		ALTERNATIVE NAME				SUB-AREA
Ⓐ Ⓥ	**Knockmealdown**		*Ir: Cnoc Mhaoldomhnaigh, 'hill of Maoldomhnach'*				

HEIGHT METRES	COUNTY	1:50K MAP NO.	MAP GRID REF	PROMINENCE	HEIGHT RANK	MV RATING	DATE CLIMBED
794	Tipperary/Waterford	74	S057₉₇ 084₁₀	682m	44	7.8	

CLASSIFICATION	MOUNTAIN NAME		ALTERNATIVE NAME				SUB-AREA
Ⓐ Ⓥ	**Knockmoylan**		*Ir: Cnoc Maoláin, 'hill of the little round or bald place'*				

HEIGHT METRES	COUNTY	1:50K MAP NO.	MAP GRID REF	PROMINENCE	HEIGHT RANK	MV RATING	DATE CLIMBED
768	Tipperary	74	S057₉₈ 093₃₆	33m	60	7.2	

CLASSIFICATION	MOUNTAIN NAME		ALTERNATIVE NAME				SUB-AREA
Ⓐ Ⓥ	**Knocknafallia**		*Ir: Cnoc na Faille, 'hill of the cliff'*				

HEIGHT METRES	COUNTY	1:50K MAP NO.	MAP GRID REF	PROMINENCE	HEIGHT RANK	MV RATING	DATE CLIMBED
668	Waterford	74	S090₀₉ 076₁₂	153m	154	7.3	

CLASSIFICATION	MOUNTAIN NAME		ALTERNATIVE NAME				SUB-AREA
Ⓐ Ⓥ	**Sugarloaf Hill**		*Ir: Cnoc na gCloch, 'hill of the stones'*				

HEIGHT METRES	COUNTY	1:50K MAP NO.	MAP GRID REF	PROMINENCE	HEIGHT RANK	MV RATING	DATE CLIMBED
663	Tipperary/Waterford	74	S039₇₀ 104₇₉	118m	166	7.1	

CLASSIFICATION	MOUNTAIN NAME		ALTERNATIVE NAME				SUB-AREA
Ⓐ Ⓥ	**Knocknagnauv**		*Ir: Cnoc na gCnámh, 'hill of the bones'*				

HEIGHT METRES	COUNTY	1:50K MAP NO.	MAP GRID REF	PROMINENCE	HEIGHT RANK	MV RATING	DATE CLIMBED
655.1*	Tipperary/Waterford	74	S081₀₇ 083₀₉	60m	176	6.7	

CLASSIFICATION	MOUNTAIN NAME		ALTERNATIVE NAME				SUB-AREA
Ⓐ Ⓥ	**Knockshanahullion**		*Ir: Cnoc Seanchuillinn, 'hill of the old holly'*				

HEIGHT METRES	COUNTY	1:50K MAP NO.	MAP GRID REF	PROMINENCE	HEIGHT RANK	MV RATING	DATE CLIMBED
652	Tipperary	74	R999₅₆ 104₄₃	317m	183	6.7	

CLASSIFICATION	MOUNTAIN NAME		ALTERNATIVE NAME				SUB-AREA
Ⓐ Ⓥ	**Knocknalougha**		*Ir: Cnoc na Loiche, 'hill of the lake'*				

HEIGHT METRES	COUNTY	1:50K MAP NO.	MAP GRID REF	PROMINENCE	HEIGHT RANK	MV RATING	DATE CLIMBED
630	Tipperary/Waterford	74	S019₄₇ 100₁₅	85m	223	6.3	

CLASSIFICATION	MOUNTAIN NAME		ALTERNATIVE NAME				SUB-AREA
Ⓐ	**Knockmeal**		*Ir: Seisceann na Maoile, 'marsh of the bare hill'*				

HEIGHT METRES	COUNTY	1:50K MAP NO.	MAP GRID REF	PROMINENCE	HEIGHT RANK	MV RATING	DATE CLIMBED
559.5*	Tipperary/Waterford	74	S102₄₇ 083₄₁	58m	336	7.0	

CLASSIFICATION	MOUNTAIN NAME		ALTERNATIVE NAME				SUB-AREA
Ⓐ	**Crohan West**		*Ir: Cruachán, 'little stack'*				

HEIGHT METRES	COUNTY	1:50K MAP NO.	MAP GRID REF	PROMINENCE	HEIGHT RANK	MV RATING	DATE CLIMBED
521	Tipperary	74	S096₇₃ 102₀₀	76m	402	7.2	

CLASSIFICATION	MOUNTAIN NAME		ALTERNATIVE NAME			SUB-AREA	
Ⓐ	**Farbreaga**		*Ir: Fear Bréige, 'false man'*				
HEIGHT METRES	COUNTY	1:50K MAP NO.	MAP GRID REF	PROMINENCE	HEIGHT RANK	MV RATING	DATE CLIMBED
518.0*	Tipperary	74	R967₉₈ 091₆₁ 73m		407	5.1	

Knockmealdown viewed from the wall crossing the summit of Knocknagnauv

MAAMTURKS

CLASSIFICATION	MOUNTAIN NAME		ALTERNATIVE NAME			SUB-AREA	
Ⓐ Ⓥ	**Binn idir an dá Log**		*Means 'peak between the two hollows'*				
HEIGHT METRES	COUNTY	1:50K MAP NO.	MAP GRID REF	PROMINENCE	HEIGHT RANK	MV RATING	DATE CLIMBED
702	Galway	37	L888₂₀ 528₂₇ 644m		107	9.2	

CLASSIFICATION	MOUNTAIN NAME		ALTERNATIVE NAME			SUB-AREA	
Ⓐ Ⓥ	**Letterbreckaun**		*Ir: Binn Bhriocáin. Means 'Brecan's peak'*				
HEIGHT METRES	COUNTY	1:50K MAP NO.	MAP GRID REF	PROMINENCE	HEIGHT RANK	MV RATING	DATE CLIMBED
667	Galway	37	L856₅₅ 550₉₇ 322m		157	8.9	

CLASSIFICATION	MOUNTAIN NAME		ALTERNATIVE NAME			SUB-AREA	
Ⓐ Ⓥ	**Binn Mhór**		*Means 'great peak'*				
HEIGHT METRES	COUNTY	1:50K MAP NO.	MAP GRID REF	PROMINENCE	HEIGHT RANK	MV RATING	DATE CLIMBED
661	Galway	44	L918₄₁ 493₅₅ 406m		168	8.0	

CLASSIFICATION	MOUNTAIN NAME		ALTERNATIVE NAME				SUB-AREA
A VL	**Binn idir an dá Log SE Top**		*Means 'peak between the two hollows'*				

HEIGHT METRES	COUNTY	1:50K MAP NO.	MAP GRID REF	PROMINENCE	HEIGHT RANK	MV RATING	DATE CLIMBED
659	Galway	37	L893₉₇ 525₈₁	31m	170	9.1	

CLASSIFICATION	MOUNTAIN NAME		ALTERNATIVE NAME				SUB-AREA
A VL	**Binn Chaonaigh**		*Means 'peak of moss'*				

HEIGHT METRES	COUNTY	1:50K MAP NO.	MAP GRID REF	PROMINENCE	HEIGHT RANK	MV RATING	DATE CLIMBED
633	Galway	37	L900₃₇ 515₆₂	108m	219	8.6	

CLASSIFICATION	MOUNTAIN NAME		ALTERNATIVE NAME				SUB-AREA
A VL	**Mullach Glas**		*Means 'grey/green summit'*				

HEIGHT METRES	COUNTY	1:50K MAP NO.	MAP GRID REF	PROMINENCE	HEIGHT RANK	MV RATING	DATE CLIMBED
622	Galway	45	L937₄₈ 492₄₆	87m	233	8.6	

CLASSIFICATION	MOUNTAIN NAME		ALTERNATIVE NAME				SUB-AREA
A VL	**Leenaun Hill**		*Ir: An Meall Dubh, 'black knoll'*				

HEIGHT METRES	COUNTY	1:50K MAP NO.	MAP GRID REF	PROMINENCE	HEIGHT RANK	MV RATING	DATE CLIMBED
618	Galway	37	L874₀₀ 593₀₀	363m	240	8.5	

CLASSIFICATION	MOUNTAIN NAME		ALTERNATIVE NAME				SUB-AREA
VL	**Binn Mhairg**		*Means 'peak of woe'*				

HEIGHT METRES	COUNTY	1:50K MAP NO.	MAP GRID REF	PROMINENCE	HEIGHT RANK	MV RATING	DATE CLIMBED
612	Galway	37	L902₅₅ 520₂₆	15m	245	9.2	

The main Maamturks ridge from Binn Bhriocáin North-east Top

Knocknahillion's rocky summit

CLASSIFICATION	MOUNTAIN NAME		ALTERNATIVE NAME			SUB-AREA	
A VL	**Corcogemore**		*Ir: Corcóg, means 'cone' or 'beehive'*				
HEIGHT METRES	COUNTY	1:50K MAP NO.	MAP GRID REF	PROMINENCE	HEIGHT RANK	MV RATING	DATE CLIMBED
609	Galway	45	L952₅₉ 491₄₇	221m	249	8.7	

CLASSIFICATION	MOUNTAIN NAME		ALTERNATIVE NAME			SUB-AREA	
A VL	**Knocknahillion**		*Ir: Cnoc na hUilleann, means 'hill of Uillinn Thiar'*				
HEIGHT METRES	COUNTY	1:50K MAP NO.	MAP GRID REF	PROMINENCE	HEIGHT RANK	MV RATING	DATE CLIMBED
607	Galway	37	L870₃₆ 537₅₆	152m	253	9.4	

CLASSIFICATION	MOUNTAIN NAME		ALTERNATIVE NAME			SUB-AREA	
VL	**Binn Bhriocáin NE Top**		*Means 'Brecan's peak'*				
HEIGHT METRES	COUNTY	1:50K MAP NO.	MAP GRID REF	PROMINENCE	HEIGHT RANK	MV RATING	DATE CLIMBED
603	Galway	37	L861₇₉ 554₅₇	28m	257	9.4	

CLASSIFICATION	MOUNTAIN NAME		ALTERNATIVE NAME			SUB-AREA	
A	**Búcán**		*Means 'spur'*				
HEIGHT METRES	COUNTY	1:50K MAP NO.	MAP GRID REF	PROMINENCE	HEIGHT RANK	MV RATING	DATE CLIMBED
550	Galway	37	L852₀₀ 607₀₀	45m	350	8.3	

CLASSIFICATION	MOUNTAIN NAME		ALTERNATIVE NAME			SUB-AREA	
A	**Knocknahillion N Top**		*Ir: Cnoc na hUilleann, means 'hill of Uillinn Thiar'*				
HEIGHT METRES	COUNTY	1:50K MAP NO.	MAP GRID REF	PROMINENCE	HEIGHT RANK	MV RATING	DATE CLIMBED
541	Galway	37	L871₃₇ 545₀₇	36m	365	9.3	

MACGILLYCUDDY'S REEKS

CLASSIFICATION	MOUNTAIN NAME	ALTERNATIVE NAME			SUB-AREA	
Ⓐ Ⓥ	**Carrauntoohil**	*Ir: Corrán Tuathail, 'Tuathal's sickle'*				

HEIGHT METRES	COUNTY	1:50K MAP NO.	MAP GRID REF	PROMINENCE	HEIGHT RANK	MV RATING	DATE CLIMBED
1,038.6*	Kerry	78	V803$_{63}$ 844$_{21}$	1,038.6*	1	8.3	

CLASSIFICATION	MOUNTAIN NAME	ALTERNATIVE NAME			SUB-AREA	
Ⓐ Ⓥ	**Beenkeragh**	*Ir: Binn Chaorach, 'mountain of sheep'*				

HEIGHT METRES	COUNTY	1:50K MAP NO.	MAP GRID REF	PROMINENCE	HEIGHT RANK	MV RATING	DATE CLIMBED
1,007.9*	Kerry	78	V801$_{39}$ 852$_{45}$	91m	2	8.9	

CLASSIFICATION	MOUNTAIN NAME	ALTERNATIVE NAME			SUB-AREA	
Ⓐ Ⓥ	**Caher**	*Ir: Cathair, 'stone fort'*				

HEIGHT METRES	COUNTY	1:50K MAP NO.	MAP GRID REF	PROMINENCE	HEIGHT RANK	MV RATING	DATE CLIMBED
1,000.0*	Kerry	78	V792$_{61}$ 838$_{91}$	99.8m	3	8.8	

CLASSIFICATION	MOUNTAIN NAME	ALTERNATIVE NAME			SUB-AREA	
Ⓐ Ⓥ	**Knocknapeasta**	*Ir: Cnoc na Péiste, 'hill of the serpent/monster'*				

HEIGHT METRES	COUNTY	1:50K MAP NO.	MAP GRID REF	PROMINENCE	HEIGHT RANK	MV RATING	DATE CLIMBED
988	Kerry	78	V835$_{87}$ 841$_{78}$	253m	4	9.3	

CLASSIFICATION	MOUNTAIN NAME	ALTERNATIVE NAME			SUB-AREA	
Ⓥ	**Caher West Top**	*Ir: Cathair, 'stone fort'*				

HEIGHT METRES	COUNTY	1:50K MAP NO.	MAP GRID REF	PROMINENCE	HEIGHT RANK	MV RATING	DATE CLIMBED
973.4*	Kerry	78	V789$_{90}$ 840$_{04}$	24m	5	8.9	

CLASSIFICATION	MOUNTAIN NAME	ALTERNATIVE NAME			SUB-AREA	
Ⓐ Ⓥ	**Maolán Buí**	*Means 'yellow/golden round knoll'*				

HEIGHT METRES	COUNTY	1:50K MAP NO.	MAP GRID REF	PROMINENCE	HEIGHT RANK	MV RATING	DATE CLIMBED
973	Kerry	78	V832$_{10}$ 838$_{16}$	38m	6	9.2	

CLASSIFICATION	MOUNTAIN NAME	ALTERNATIVE NAME			SUB-AREA	
Ⓐ Ⓥ	**Cnoc an Chuillinn**	*Means 'hill of the steep slope'*				

HEIGHT METRES	COUNTY	1:50K MAP NO.	MAP GRID REF	PROMINENCE	HEIGHT RANK	MV RATING	DATE CLIMBED
958	Kerry	78	V823$_{44}$ 833$_{37}$	53m	7	9.0	

CLASSIFICATION	MOUNTAIN NAME	ALTERNATIVE NAME			SUB-AREA	
Ⓐ Ⓥ	**The Bones**	*Previously Carrauntoohil Tooth in MV*				

HEIGHT METRES	COUNTY	1:50K MAP NO.	MAP GRID REF	PROMINENCE	HEIGHT RANK	MV RATING	DATE CLIMBED
956.5*	Kerry	78	V800$_{70}$ 846$_{80}$	37m	8	8.8	

CLASSIFICATION	MOUNTAIN NAME	ALTERNATIVE NAME			SUB-AREA	
Ⓐ Ⓥ	**The Big Gun**	*Ir: An Gunna Mór, 'the big gun'*				

HEIGHT METRES	COUNTY	1:50K MAP NO.	MAP GRID REF	PROMINENCE	HEIGHT RANK	MV RATING	DATE CLIMBED
939	Kerry	78	V840$_{69}$ 845$_{00}$	74m	10	9.4	

The eastern ridge of MacGillycuddy's Reeks, heading for Cnoc an Chuillinn

The ridge to Caher

CLASSIFICATION	MOUNTAIN NAME		ALTERNATIVE NAME					SUB-AREA
A VL	**Cnoc na dTarbh**		*Means 'hill of the bulls'*					
HEIGHT METRES	COUNTY	1:50K MAP NO.	MAP GRID REF	PROMINENCE	HEIGHT RANK	MV RATING	DATE CLIMBED	
655	Kerry	78	V862₃₄ 849₉₅	60m	175	6.7		

CLASSIFICATION	MOUNTAIN NAME		ALTERNATIVE NAME					SUB-AREA
VL	**Hag's Tooth**		*Ir: Stumpa an tSaimh, 'stump of the sorrel'*					
HEIGHT METRES	COUNTY	1:50K MAP NO.	MAP GRID REF	PROMINENCE	HEIGHT RANK	MV RATING	DATE CLIMBED	
650	Kerry	78	V809₃₈ 850₅₅	15m	187	9.4		

CLASSIFICATION	MOUNTAIN NAME		ALTERNATIVE NAME					SUB-AREA
A	**Brassel Mountain**		*Ir: Cnoc Breasail, 'hill of raddle'*					
HEIGHT METRES	COUNTY	1:50K MAP NO.	MAP GRID REF	PROMINENCE	HEIGHT RANK	MV RATING	DATE CLIMBED	
575	Kerry	78	V830₀₀ 823₀₀	50m	309	8.2		

CLASSIFICATION	MOUNTAIN NAME		ALTERNATIVE NAME					SUB-AREA
A	**Skregbeg**		*Ir: Screig Bheag, 'little rocky outcrop'*					
HEIGHT METRES	COUNTY	1:50K MAP NO.	MAP GRID REF	PROMINENCE	HEIGHT RANK	MV RATING	DATE CLIMBED	
573	Kerry	78	V787₂₃ 874₂₆	78m	313	7.5		

Lough Callee and Lough Gouragh at the head of the Hag's Glen

CLASSIFICATION	MOUNTAIN NAME	ALTERNATIVE NAME		SUB-AREA
Ⓐ Ⓥ	**Mangerton**	*Ir: An Mhangarta, poss. 'the long-haired (mountain)'*		

HEIGHT METRES	COUNTY	1:50K MAP NO.	MAP GRID REF	PROMINENCE	HEIGHT RANK	MV RATING	DATE CLIMBED
839	Kerry	78	V980₃₆ 807₈₅	584m	25	7.7	

CLASSIFICATION	MOUNTAIN NAME	ALTERNATIVE NAME		SUB-AREA
Ⓐ Ⓥ	**Mangerton N Top**	*Ir: An Mhangarta, poss. 'the long-haired (mountain)'*		

HEIGHT METRES	COUNTY	1:50K MAP NO.	MAP GRID REF	PROMINENCE	HEIGHT RANK	MV RATING	DATE CLIMBED
782	Kerry	78	V984₆₆ 818₆₈	67m	55	8.1	

CLASSIFICATION	MOUNTAIN NAME	ALTERNATIVE NAME		SUB-AREA
Ⓐ Ⓥ	**Stoompa**	*Ir: Stumpa, 'stump'*		

HEIGHT METRES	COUNTY	1:50K MAP NO.	MAP GRID REF	PROMINENCE	HEIGHT RANK	MV RATING	DATE CLIMBED
705	Kerry	79	W006₄₈ 817₈₂	90m	104	7.8	

CLASSIFICATION	MOUNTAIN NAME	ALTERNATIVE NAME		SUB-AREA
Ⓥ	**Dromderalough NE Top**	*Ir: Drom idir Dhá Loch, 'ridge between two lakes'*		

HEIGHT METRES	COUNTY	1:50K MAP NO.	MAP GRID REF	PROMINENCE	HEIGHT RANK	MV RATING	DATE CLIMBED
654	Kerry	78	V969₅₄ 795₈₆	29m	179	6.4	

CLASSIFICATION	MOUNTAIN NAME	ALTERNATIVE NAME		SUB-AREA
Ⓐ Ⓥ	**Dromderalough**	*Ir: Drom idir Dhá Loch, 'ridge between two lakes'*		

HEIGHT METRES	COUNTY	1:50K MAP NO.	MAP GRID REF	PROMINENCE	HEIGHT RANK	MV RATING	DATE CLIMBED
650	Kerry	78	V960₉₄ 790₁₃	45m	188	7.5	

CLASSIFICATION	MOUNTAIN NAME	ALTERNATIVE NAME		SUB-AREA
Ⓐ Ⓥ	**Crohane**	*Ir: An Cruachán, 'little stack'*		

HEIGHT METRES	COUNTY	1:50K MAP NO.	MAP GRID REF	PROMINENCE	HEIGHT RANK	MV RATING	DATE CLIMBED
650	Kerry	79	W049₇₁ 829₆₇	385m	189	7.7	

CLASSIFICATION	MOUNTAIN NAME	ALTERNATIVE NAME		SUB-AREA
Ⓐ Ⓥ	**Knockbrack**	*Ir: An Cnoc Breac, 'speckled hill'*		

HEIGHT METRES	COUNTY	1:50K MAP NO.	MAP GRID REF	PROMINENCE	HEIGHT RANK	MV RATING	DATE CLIMBED
610	Kerry	78	V953₅₈ 779₆₆	45m	248	7.9	

CLASSIFICATION	MOUNTAIN NAME	ALTERNATIVE NAME		SUB-AREA
Ⓥ	**Stoompa E Top**	*Ir: Stumpa, 'stump'*		

HEIGHT METRES	COUNTY	1:50K MAP NO.	MAP GRID REF	PROMINENCE	HEIGHT RANK	MV RATING	DATE CLIMBED
608	Kerry	79	W017₅₉ 819₅₂	23m	250	7.7	

CLASSIFICATION	MOUNTAIN NAME	ALTERNATIVE NAME		SUB-AREA
Ⓐ	**Peakeen Mtn**	*Ir: Péicín, 'boundary marker'*		

HEIGHT METRES	COUNTY	1:50K MAP NO.	MAP GRID REF	PROMINENCE	HEIGHT RANK	MV RATING	DATE CLIMBED
555	Kerry	78	V903₄₄ 764₉₉	280m	341	8.0	

CLASSIFICATION	MOUNTAIN NAME		ALTERNATIVE NAME			SUB-AREA	
Ⓐ	**Knockrower**		*Ir: Cnoc Ramhar, 'fat hill'*				
HEIGHT METRES	COUNTY	1:50K MAP NO.	MAP GRID REF	PROMINENCE	HEIGHT RANK	MV RATING	DATE CLIMBED
554	Kerry	78	V937₄₈ 784₅₃ 59m		347	7.6	

CLASSIFICATION	MOUNTAIN NAME		ALTERNATIVE NAME			SUB-AREA	
Ⓐ	**Peakeen Mtn W Top**		*Ir: Péicín, 'boundary marker'*				
HEIGHT METRES	COUNTY	1:50K MAP NO.	MAP GRID REF	PROMINENCE	HEIGHT RANK	MV RATING	DATE CLIMBED
541	Kerry	78	V889₅₃ 764₈₁ 93m		366	6.8	

CLASSIFICATION	MOUNTAIN NAME		ALTERNATIVE NAME			SUB-AREA	
Ⓐ	**Torc Mtn**		*Ir: Sliabh Torc, 'mountain of wild boar'*				
HEIGHT METRES	COUNTY	1:50K MAP NO.	MAP GRID REF	PROMINENCE	HEIGHT RANK	MV RATING	DATE CLIMBED
535	Kerry	78	V955₇₄ 839₃₅ 300m		375	6.9	

CLASSIFICATION	MOUNTAIN NAME		ALTERNATIVE NAME			SUB-AREA	
Ⓐ	**Knockanaguish**		*Ir: Cnoc an Uaignis, 'hill of the solitude'*				
HEIGHT METRES	COUNTY	1:50K MAP NO.	MAP GRID REF	PROMINENCE	HEIGHT RANK	MV RATING	DATE CLIMBED
509	Kerry	78	V919₃₀ 768₅₇ 178m		429	7.9	

Lough Frhough beneath Mangerton's northern cliffs

CLASSIFICATION	MOUNTAIN NAME		ALTERNATIVE NAME				SUB-AREA
A VL	**Slieve Donard**		*Ir: Sliabh Dónairt, 'mountain of (St) Domhangart'*				
HEIGHT METRES	COUNTY	1:50K MAP NO.	MAP GRID REF	PROMINENCE	HEIGHT RANK	MV RATING	DATE CLIMBED
850	Down	29	J357₉₆ 276₉₀	822m	19	7.7	

CLASSIFICATION	MOUNTAIN NAME		ALTERNATIVE NAME				SUB-AREA
A VL	**Slieve Commedagh**		*Ir: Sliabh Coimhéideach, 'watching/guarding mtn'*				
HEIGHT METRES	COUNTY	1:50K MAP NO.	MAP GRID REF	PROMINENCE	HEIGHT RANK	MV RATING	DATE CLIMBED
767	Down	29	J346₁₀ 286₁₆	180m	62	8.3	

CLASSIFICATION	MOUNTAIN NAME		ALTERNATIVE NAME				SUB-AREA
A VL	**Slieve Binnian**		*Ir: Sliabh Binneáin, 'mountain of the small peak'*				
HEIGHT METRES	COUNTY	1:50K MAP NO.	MAP GRID REF	PROMINENCE	HEIGHT RANK	MV RATING	DATE CLIMBED
747	Down	29	J320₆₅ 233₅₅	283m	77	8.6	

CLASSIFICATION	MOUNTAIN NAME		ALTERNATIVE NAME				SUB-AREA
A VL	**Slieve Bearnagh**		*Ir: Sliabh Bearnach, 'gapped mountain'*				
HEIGHT METRES	COUNTY	1:50K MAP NO.	MAP GRID REF	PROMINENCE	HEIGHT RANK	MV RATING	DATE CLIMBED
739	Down	29	J313₁₆ 280₃₅	304m	82	8.9	

CLASSIFICATION	MOUNTAIN NAME		ALTERNATIVE NAME				SUB-AREA
A VL	**Slieve Meelbeg**		*Ir: Sliabh Míol Beag, 'little mountain of the ants'*				
HEIGHT METRES	COUNTY	1:50K MAP NO.	MAP GRID REF	PROMINENCE	HEIGHT RANK	MV RATING	DATE CLIMBED
708	Down	29	J300₇₅ 279₁₈	193m	102	7.6	

CLASSIFICATION	MOUNTAIN NAME		ALTERNATIVE NAME				SUB-AREA
A VL	**Slievelamagan**		*Ir: Sliabh Lámhagáin, 'creeping/crawling mtn'*				
HEIGHT METRES	COUNTY	1:50K MAP NO.	MAP GRID REF	PROMINENCE	HEIGHT RANK	MV RATING	DATE CLIMBED
704	Down	29	J328₉₇ 260₅₂	199m	105	8.5	

CLASSIFICATION	MOUNTAIN NAME		ALTERNATIVE NAME				SUB-AREA
A VL	**Slieve Meelmore**		*Ir: Sliabh Míol Mór, 'big mountain of the ants'*				
HEIGHT METRES	COUNTY	1:50K MAP NO.	MAP GRID REF	PROMINENCE	HEIGHT RANK	MV RATING	DATE CLIMBED
680	Down	29	J305₉₄ 287₀₂	109m	135	7.7	

CLASSIFICATION	MOUNTAIN NAME		ALTERNATIVE NAME				SUB-AREA
A VL	**Slieve Binnian N Top**		*Ir: Sliabh Binneáin, 'mountain of the small peak'*				
HEIGHT METRES	COUNTY	1:50K MAP NO.	MAP GRID REF	PROMINENCE	HEIGHT RANK	MV RATING	DATE CLIMBED
678	Down	29	J316₉₄ 245₁₈	53m	141	7.6	

CLASSIFICATION	MOUNTAIN NAME		ALTERNATIVE NAME				SUB-AREA
A VL	**Slieve Muck**		*Ir: Sliabh Muc, 'mountain of the pigs'*				
HEIGHT METRES	COUNTY	1:50K MAP NO.	MAP GRID REF	PROMINENCE	HEIGHT RANK	MV RATING	DATE CLIMBED
674	Down	29	J281₁₂ 249₉₉	159m	147	8.5	

Swirling cloud on Slievelamagan partially obscuring Slieve Binnian

CLASSIFICATION	MOUNTAIN NAME		ALTERNATIVE NAME			SUB-AREA	
ⓋⓁ	**Slieve Binnian N Tor**		*Ir: Sliabh Binneáin, 'mountain of the small peak'*				
HEIGHT METRES	COUNTY	1:50K MAP NO.	MAP GRID REF	PROMINENCE	HEIGHT RANK	MV RATING	DATE CLIMBED
670	Down	29	J319₇₁ 246₀₆	15m	152	9.2	

CLASSIFICATION	MOUNTAIN NAME		ALTERNATIVE NAME			SUB-AREA	
Ⓐ ⓋⓁ	**Chimney Rock Mtn**		*Ir: Sliabh an Aoire (?), 'mountain of the shepherd'*				
HEIGHT METRES	COUNTY	1:50K MAP NO.	MAP GRID REF	PROMINENCE	HEIGHT RANK	MV RATING	DATE CLIMBED
656	Down	29	J364₀₉ 257₂₁	131m	174	8.5	

CLASSIFICATION	MOUNTAIN NAME		ALTERNATIVE NAME			SUB-AREA	
Ⓐ ⓋⓁ	**Cove Mtn**						
HEIGHT METRES	COUNTY	1:50K MAP NO.	MAP GRID REF	PROMINENCE	HEIGHT RANK	MV RATING	DATE CLIMBED
655	Down	29	J336₆₆ 270₈₄	100m	177	7.6	

CLASSIFICATION	MOUNTAIN NAME		ALTERNATIVE NAME			SUB-AREA	
ⓋⓁ	**Slieve Corragh**		*Ir: Sliabh Corrach, 'rugged/pointed mountain'*				
HEIGHT METRES	COUNTY	1:50K MAP NO.	MAP GRID REF	PROMINENCE	HEIGHT RANK	MV RATING	DATE CLIMBED
640	Down	29	J337₀₅ 286₁₁	15m	206	6.8	

CLASSIFICATION	MOUNTAIN NAME		ALTERNATIVE NAME			SUB-AREA	
Ⓐ ⓋⓁ	**Eagle Mtn**		*Ir: Sliabh an Iolair, 'mountain of the eagle'*				
HEIGHT METRES	COUNTY	1:50K MAP NO.	MAP GRID REF	PROMINENCE	HEIGHT RANK	MV RATING	DATE CLIMBED
638	Down	29	J244₉₂ 229₇₇	263m	211	7.9	

The Mourne Wall on the summit of Slieve Meelbeg; Doan and Binnian are in the background

Cloud over Slieve Binnian's magnificent and unique tors

CLASSIFICATION	MOUNTAIN NAME		ALTERNATIVE NAME				SUB-AREA
VL	**Slieve Binnian E Top**		*Ir: Sliabh Binneáin, 'mountain of the small peak'*				
HEIGHT METRES	COUNTY	1:50K MAP NO.	MAP GRID REF	PROMINENCE	HEIGHT RANK	MV RATING	DATE CLIMBED
630	Down	29	J326$_{60}$ 231$_{69}$	15m	224	7.5	

CLASSIFICATION	MOUNTAIN NAME		ALTERNATIVE NAME				SUB-AREA
A VL	**Shanlieve**		*Ir: Seanshliabh, 'old mountain'*				
HEIGHT METRES	COUNTY	1:50K MAP NO.	MAP GRID REF	PROMINENCE	HEIGHT RANK	MV RATING	DATE CLIMBED
626	Down	29	J240$_{68}$ 226$_{69}$	31m	230	7.4	

CLASSIFICATION	MOUNTAIN NAME		ALTERNATIVE NAME				SUB-AREA
A VL	**Slieve Loughshannagh**		*Ir: Sliabh Loch Seannach, 'mtn of Lough Shannagh'*				
HEIGHT METRES	COUNTY	1:50K MAP NO.	MAP GRID REF	PROMINENCE	HEIGHT RANK	MV RATING	DATE CLIMBED
619	Down	29	J294$_{60}$ 272$_{03}$	104m	239	7.1	

CLASSIFICATION	MOUNTAIN NAME		ALTERNATIVE NAME				SUB-AREA
A	**Doan**		*Ir: Dún Maol Chobha, 'Maol Chobha's fort'*				
HEIGHT METRES	COUNTY	1:50K MAP NO.	MAP GRID REF	PROMINENCE	HEIGHT RANK	MV RATING	DATE CLIMBED
593	Down	29	J302$_{81}$ 262$_{21}$	119m	281	7.9	

CLASSIFICATION	MOUNTAIN NAME		ALTERNATIVE NAME				SUB-AREA
A	**Slieve Beg**		*Ir: Sliabh Beag, 'little mountain'*				
HEIGHT METRES	COUNTY	1:50K MAP NO.	MAP GRID REF	PROMINENCE	HEIGHT RANK	MV RATING	DATE CLIMBED
590	Down	29	J340$_{32}$ 275$_{94}$	35m	298	7.6	

CLASSIFICATION	MOUNTAIN NAME		ALTERNATIVE NAME				SUB-AREA
A	**Carn Mtn**		*Ir: Sliabh an Chairn, 'mountain of the cairn'*				
HEIGHT METRES	COUNTY	1:50K MAP NO.	MAP GRID REF	PROMINENCE	HEIGHT RANK	MV RATING	DATE CLIMBED
588	Down	29	J287$_{92}$ 260$_{14}$	53m	291	6.9	

CLASSIFICATION	MOUNTAIN NAME		ALTERNATIVE NAME				SUB-AREA
A	**Slievenaglogh**		*Ir:Sliabh na gCloch, 'mtn of the stones/rocks'*				
HEIGHT METRES	COUNTY	1:50K MAP NO.	MAP GRID REF	PROMINENCE	HEIGHT RANK	MV RATING	DATE CLIMBED
586	Down	29	J327$_{83}$ 291$_{07}$	41m	295	7.1	

CLASSIFICATION	MOUNTAIN NAME		ALTERNATIVE NAME				SUB-AREA
A	**Slievemoughanmore**						
HEIGHT METRES	COUNTY	1:50K MAP NO.	MAP GRID REF	PROMINENCE	HEIGHT RANK	MV RATING	DATE CLIMBED
560	Down	29	J249$_{59}$ 240$_{95}$	154m	337	6.9	

CLASSIFICATION	MOUNTAIN NAME		ALTERNATIVE NAME				SUB-AREA
A	**Pigeon Rock Mtn**		*Ir: Droim Lao, 'ridge of the calf'*				
HEIGHT METRES	COUNTY	1:50K MAP NO.	MAP GRID REF	PROMINENCE	HEIGHT RANK	MV RATING	DATE CLIMBED
534	Down	29	J261$_{32}$ 250$_{30}$	139m	379	7.2	

CLASSIFICATION	MOUNTAIN NAME	ALTERNATIVE NAME	SUB-AREA
A	**Slieve Croob**	*Ir: Sliabh Crúibe, 'mountain of the hoof'*	

HEIGHT METRES	COUNTY	1:50K MAP NO.	MAP GRID REF	PROMINENCE	HEIGHT RANK	MV RATING	DATE CLIMBED
534	Down	20	J318₄₅ 453₇₈	439m	380	6.0	

CLASSIFICATION	MOUNTAIN NAME	ALTERNATIVE NAME	SUB-AREA
A	**Ben Crom**	*Ir: Binn Crom or Beann Chrom, 'curved/stooped peak'*	

HEIGHT METRES	COUNTY	1:50K MAP NO.	MAP GRID REF	PROMINENCE	HEIGHT RANK	MV RATING	DATE CLIMBED
526	Down	29	J313₀₀ 260₀₀	81m	396	8.1	

CLASSIFICATION	MOUNTAIN NAME	ALTERNATIVE NAME	SUB-AREA
A	**Rocky Mtn**	*Ir: Sliabh na gCloch, 'mountain of the stones'*	

HEIGHT METRES	COUNTY	1:50K MAP NO.	MAP GRID REF	PROMINENCE	HEIGHT RANK	MV RATING	DATE CLIMBED
524	Down	29	J350₇₁ 252₅₅	60m	398	6.8	

CLASSIFICATION	MOUNTAIN NAME	ALTERNATIVE NAME	SUB-AREA
A	**Cock Mtn**	*Ir: Sliabh an Choiligh, 'mountain of the cock'*	

HEIGHT METRES	COUNTY	1:50K MAP NO.	MAP GRID REF	PROMINENCE	HEIGHT RANK	MV RATING	DATE CLIMBED
504	Down	29	J253₅₇ 268₄₁	130m	441	7.2	

CLASSIFICATION	MOUNTAIN NAME	ALTERNATIVE NAME	SUB-AREA
A	**Butter Mtn**	*Ir: Sliabh an Ime, 'mountain of the butter'*	

HEIGHT METRES	COUNTY	1:50K MAP NO.	MAP GRID REF	PROMINENCE	HEIGHT RANK	MV RATING	DATE CLIMBED
500	Down	29	J274₈₀ 279₇₅	95m	453	5.8	

Doan and the Silent Valley in winter

The Ben Lugmore ridge heading for Ben Bury

MWEELREA MOUNTAINS

CLASSIFICATION	MOUNTAIN NAME		ALTERNATIVE NAME			SUB-AREA	
Ⓐ ⓋⓁ	**Mweelrea**		Ir: Cnoc Maol Réidh, 'bald hill with the smooth top'				
HEIGHT METRES	**COUNTY**	**1:50K MAP NO.**	**MAP GRID REF**	**PROMINENCE**	**HEIGHT RANK**	**MV RATING**	**DATE CLIMBED**
814	Mayo	37	L789₈₃ 668₁₀	779m	33	9.2	

CLASSIFICATION	MOUNTAIN NAME		ALTERNATIVE NAME			SUB-AREA	
Ⓐ ⓋⓁ	**Ben Lugmore**		Ir: Binn Log Mhór, 'peak of the big hollow'				
HEIGHT METRES	**COUNTY**	**1:50K MAP NO.**	**MAP GRID REF**	**PROMINENCE**	**HEIGHT RANK**	**MV RATING**	**DATE CLIMBED**
803	Mayo	37	L811₇₃ 673₇₉	158m	37	9.5	

CLASSIFICATION	MOUNTAIN NAME		ALTERNATIVE NAME			SUB-AREA	
Ⓐ ⓋⓁ	**Ben Bury**		Ir: Ucht an Chreagáin, 'breast of the little crag'				
HEIGHT METRES	**COUNTY**	**1:50K MAP NO.**	**MAP GRID REF**	**PROMINENCE**	**HEIGHT RANK**	**MV RATING**	**DATE CLIMBED**
795	Mayo	37	L802₄₄ 682₉₀	60m	42	9.2	

CLASSIFICATION	MOUNTAIN NAME		ALTERNATIVE NAME			SUB-AREA	
Ⓐ ⓋⓁ	**Ben Lugmore W Top**		Ir: Binn Log Mhór, 'peak of the big hollow'				
HEIGHT METRES	**COUNTY**	**1:50K MAP NO.**	**MAP GRID REF**	**PROMINENCE**	**HEIGHT RANK**	**MV RATING**	**DATE CLIMBED**
790	Mayo	37	L805₈₅ 676₇₈	47m	49	9.3	

CLASSIFICATION	MOUNTAIN NAME		ALTERNATIVE NAME			SUB-AREA	
Ⓐ ⓋⓁ	**Ben Lugmore E Top**		Ir: Binn Log Mhór, 'peak of the big hollow'				
HEIGHT METRES	**COUNTY**	**1:50K MAP NO.**	**MAP GRID REF**	**PROMINENCE**	**HEIGHT RANK**	**MV RATING**	**DATE CLIMBED**
790	Mayo	37	L815₃₅ 672₀₀	37m	50	9.5	

CLASSIFICATION	MOUNTAIN NAME	ALTERNATIVE NAME	SUB-AREA
Ⓐ Ⓥ	**Nephin**	*Ir: Néifinn, poss. 'sanctuary'*	

HEIGHT METRES	COUNTY	1:50K MAP NO.	MAP GRID REF	PROMINENCE	HEIGHT RANK	MV RATING	DATE CLIMBED
806	Mayo	23/31	G103$_{47}$ 079$_{75}$	778m	35	8.3	

CLASSIFICATION	MOUNTAIN NAME	ALTERNATIVE NAME	SUB-AREA
Ⓐ Ⓥ	**Slieve Carr**	*Ir: Corrshliabh, 'conspicuous/pointed mtn'*	

HEIGHT METRES	COUNTY	1:50K MAP NO.	MAP GRID REF	PROMINENCE	HEIGHT RANK	MV RATING	DATE CLIMBED
721	Mayo	23	F914$_{93}$ 144$_{98}$	646m	93	9.2	

CLASSIFICATION	MOUNTAIN NAME	ALTERNATIVE NAME	SUB-AREA
Ⓐ Ⓥ	**Corranabinnia**	*Ir: Coire na Binne, 'hollow of the peak'*	

HEIGHT METRES	COUNTY	1:50K MAP NO.	MAP GRID REF	PROMINENCE	HEIGHT RANK	MV RATING	DATE CLIMBED
716	Mayo	30	F903$_{07}$ 031$_{65}$	541m	97	9.2	

CLASSIFICATION	MOUNTAIN NAME	ALTERNATIVE NAME	SUB-AREA
Ⓐ Ⓥ	**Birreencorragh**	*Ir: Birín Corrach, 'rocky little spike'*	

HEIGHT METRES	COUNTY	1:50K MAP NO.	MAP GRID REF	PROMINENCE	HEIGHT RANK	MV RATING	DATE CLIMBED
698	Mayo	23/31	G024$_{56}$ 050$_{07}$	583m	110	8.9	

CLASSIFICATION	MOUNTAIN NAME	ALTERNATIVE NAME	SUB-AREA
Ⓐ Ⓥ	**Corranabinnia SW Top**	*Ir: Coire na Binne, 'hollow of the peak'*	

HEIGHT METRES	COUNTY	1:50K MAP NO.	MAP GRID REF	PROMINENCE	HEIGHT RANK	MV RATING	DATE CLIMBED
681	Mayo	30	F897$_{69}$ 026$_{21}$	56m	131	9.9	

CLASSIFICATION	MOUNTAIN NAME	ALTERNATIVE NAME	SUB-AREA
Ⓐ Ⓥ	**Glennamong**		

HEIGHT METRES	COUNTY	1:50K MAP NO.	MAP GRID REF	PROMINENCE	HEIGHT RANK	MV RATING	DATE CLIMBED
628	Mayo	23/30	F913$_{28}$ 058$_{73}$	139m	226	9.5	

CLASSIFICATION	MOUNTAIN NAME	ALTERNATIVE NAME	SUB-AREA
Ⓐ Ⓥ	**Nephin Beg**	*Ir: Néifinn Bheag, poss. 'little sanctuary'*	

HEIGHT METRES	COUNTY	1:50K MAP NO.	MAP GRID REF	PROMINENCE	HEIGHT RANK	MV RATING	DATE CLIMBED
627	Mayo	23	F931$_{97}$ 102$_{23}$	365m	227	8.3	

CLASSIFICATION	MOUNTAIN NAME	ALTERNATIVE NAME	SUB-AREA
Ⓐ	**Buckoogh**	*Ir: Boc Umhach, 'eminence rich in copper'*	

HEIGHT METRES	COUNTY	1:50K MAP NO.	MAP GRID REF	PROMINENCE	HEIGHT RANK	MV RATING	DATE CLIMBED
588	Mayo	31	F995$_{00}$ 017$_{42}$	423m	290	7.3	

CLASSIFICATION	MOUNTAIN NAME	ALTERNATIVE NAME	SUB-AREA
Ⓐ	**Bengorm**	*Ir: An Bhinn Ghorm, 'the blue peak'*	Nephin Begs

HEIGHT METRES	COUNTY	1:50K MAP NO.	MAP GRID REF	PROMINENCE	HEIGHT RANK	MV RATING	DATE CLIMBED
582	Mayo	31	F928$_{32}$ 013$_{28}$	225m	300	9.2	

The snaking ridge from Corranabinnia to Glennamong, with remote Slieve Carr on the horizon

The knife-edge ridge between Corranabinnia and the South-west Top

Beyond the cairn of the mightily named Slieve Alp lies triangular Slievemore on Achill Island

CLASSIFICATION	MOUNTAIN NAME		ALTERNATIVE NAME				SUB-AREA
Ⓐ	**Birreencorragh S Top**		*Ir: Birín Corrach, 'rocky little spike'*				Nephin Begs
HEIGHT METRES	COUNTY	1:50K MAP NO.	MAP GRID REF	PROMINENCE	HEIGHT RANK	MV RATING	DATE CLIMBED
564	Mayo	31	G024₂₇ 030₈₃	59m	328	8.4	

CLASSIFICATION	MOUNTAIN NAME		ALTERNATIVE NAME				SUB-AREA
Ⓐ	**Birreencorragh W Top**		*Ir: Birín Corrach, 'rocky little spike'*				Nephin Begs
HEIGHT METRES	COUNTY	1:50K MAP NO.	MAP GRID REF	PROMINENCE	HEIGHT RANK	MV RATING	DATE CLIMBED
551	Mayo	23/31	G014₅₇ 049₈₅	36m	349	7.4	

CLASSIFICATION	MOUNTAIN NAME		ALTERNATIVE NAME				SUB-AREA
Ⓐ	**Knockaffertagh**		*Ir: Cnoc Eachmarcaigh, 'hill of Eachmarcach'*				Nephin Begs
HEIGHT METRES	COUNTY	1:50K MAP NO.	MAP GRID REF	PROMINENCE	HEIGHT RANK	MV RATING	DATE CLIMBED
517	Mayo	23/31	G047₁₆ 048₈₆	92m	409	8.6	

CLASSIFICATION	MOUNTAIN NAME		ALTERNATIVE NAME				SUB-AREA
Ⓐ	**Claggan Mtn NE Top**		*Ir: Sliabh na Cloigne, 'mtn of the skull/skull-shaped top'*				Nephin Begs
HEIGHT METRES	COUNTY	1:50K MAP NO.	MAP GRID REF	PROMINENCE	HEIGHT RANK	MV RATING	DATE CLIMBED
501	Mayo	30	F858₆₆ 010₆₀	146m	447	7.9	

OX MOUNTAINS

CLASSIFICATION	MOUNTAIN NAME		ALTERNATIVE NAME				SUB-AREA
Ⓐ	**Knockalongy**		*Ir: Cnoc na Loinge, 'hill of the encampment'*				

HEIGHT METRES	COUNTY	1:50K MAP NO.	MAP GRID REF	PROMINENCE	HEIGHT RANK	MV RATING	DATE CLIMBED
544	Sligo	25	G504₂₈ 275₁₃ 490m		358	6.2	

CLASSIFICATION	MOUNTAIN NAME		ALTERNATIVE NAME				SUB-AREA
Ⓐ	**Annatoran**						

HEIGHT METRES	COUNTY	1:50K MAP NO.	MAP GRID REF	PROMINENCE	HEIGHT RANK	MV RATING	DATE CLIMBED
512	Sligo	24	G474₉₇ 244₈₆ 97m		422	6.0	

Knockalongy's lonely trig pillar in the Ox Mountains

Caherbarnagh summit trig pillar, North Top in the distance

CLASSIFICATION	MOUNTAIN NAME	ALTERNATIVE NAME			SUB-AREA	
Ⓐ Ⓥ	**The Paps East**	*Ir: An Dá Chích, 'the two breasts'*				
HEIGHT METRES	COUNTY	1:50K MAP NO.	MAP GRID REF	PROMINENCE	HEIGHT RANK	MV RATING	DATE CLIMBED
694	Kerry	79	W133₂₂ 855₄₃	623m	114	8.1	

CLASSIFICATION	MOUNTAIN NAME	ALTERNATIVE NAME			SUB-AREA	
Ⓐ Ⓥ	**The Paps West**	*Ir: An Dá Chích, 'the two breasts'*				
HEIGHT METRES	COUNTY	1:50K MAP NO.	MAP GRID REF	PROMINENCE	HEIGHT RANK	MV RATING	DATE CLIMBED
690	Kerry	79	W125₀₃ 855₂₈	106m	122	9.1	

CLASSIFICATION	MOUNTAIN NAME	ALTERNATIVE NAME			SUB-AREA	
Ⓐ Ⓥ	**Caherbarnagh**	*Ir: An Chathair Bhearnach, 'the gapped fort'*				
HEIGHT METRES	COUNTY	1:50K MAP NO.	MAP GRID REF	PROMINENCE	HEIGHT RANK	MV RATING	DATE CLIMBED
681	Cork	79	W191₆₁ 871₇₅	361m	132	7.2	

CLASSIFICATION	MOUNTAIN NAME	ALTERNATIVE NAME			SUB-AREA	
Ⓥ	**Caherbarnagh NW Top**	*Ir: An Chathair Bhearnach, 'the gapped fort'*				
HEIGHT METRES	COUNTY	1:50K MAP NO.	MAP GRID REF	PROMINENCE	HEIGHT RANK	MV RATING	DATE CLIMBED
668	Cork	79	W187₇₈ 876₆₃	23m	153	6.7	

CLASSIFICATION	MOUNTAIN NAME	ALTERNATIVE NAME			SUB-AREA	
Ⓐ Ⓥ	**Mullaghanish**	*Ir: Mullach an Ois, 'summit of the deer'*				
HEIGHT METRES	COUNTY	1:50K MAP NO.	MAP GRID REF	PROMINENCE	HEIGHT RANK	MV RATING	DATE CLIMBED
649	Cork/Kerry	79	W214₃₂ 817₈₃	264m	193	5.0	

CLASSIFICATION	MOUNTAIN NAME	ALTERNATIVE NAME					SUB-AREA
Ⓐ	**Knocknabro W Top**	*Ir: Cnoc na Bró, 'hill of the quern'*					
HEIGHT METRES	COUNTY	1:50K MAP NO.	MAP GRID REF	PROMINENCE	HEIGHT RANK	MV RATING	DATE CLIMBED
592	Kerry	79	W153₇₉ 853₈₉	147m	283	6.4	

CLASSIFICATION	MOUNTAIN NAME	ALTERNATIVE NAME					SUB-AREA
Ⓐ	**Knocknagowan**	*Ir: Cnoc na nGamhann, 'hill of the calves'*					
HEIGHT METRES	COUNTY	1:50K MAP NO.	MAP GRID REF	PROMINENCE	HEIGHT RANK	MV RATING	DATE CLIMBED
574	Kerry	79	W186₀₇ 850₂₀	37m	312	6.6	

CLASSIFICATION	MOUNTAIN NAME	ALTERNATIVE NAME					SUB-AREA
Ⓐ	**Coomagearlahy**						
HEIGHT METRES	COUNTY	1:50K MAP NO.	MAP GRID REF	PROMINENCE	HEIGHT RANK	MV RATING	DATE CLIMBED
506	Kerry	79	W094₉₇ 772₈₇	181m	437	4.6	

From Devilsmother looking along the ridge to Knocklaur and the Maamtrasna plateau

PARTRY/JOYCE COUNTRY

CLASSIFICATION	MOUNTAIN NAME	ALTERNATIVE NAME					SUB-AREA
Ⓐ Ⓥⓛ	**Maumtrasna**	*Ir: Mám Trasna, 'pass across'*					Partry Mtns
HEIGHT METRES	COUNTY	1:50K MAP NO.	MAP GRID REF	PROMINENCE	HEIGHT RANK	MV RATING	DATE CLIMBED
682	Mayo	38	L960₈₉ 637₄₂	607m	129	7.5	

CLASSIFICATION	MOUNTAIN NAME	ALTERNATIVE NAME					SUB-AREA
Ⓐ Ⓥⓛ	**Devilsmother**	*Ir: Binn Gharbh, 'rough peak'*					Partry Mtns
HEIGHT METRES	COUNTY	1:50K MAP NO.	MAP GRID REF	PROMINENCE	HEIGHT RANK	MV RATING	DATE CLIMBED
645	Mayo/Galway	37	L915₆₈ 624₄₇	280m	196	8.6	

CLASSIFICATION	MOUNTAIN NAME	ALTERNATIVE NAME					SUB-AREA
Ⓥⓛ	**Devilsmother N Top**	*Ir: Binn Gharbh, 'rough peak'*					Partry Mtns
HEIGHT METRES	COUNTY	1:50K MAP NO.	MAP GRID REF	PROMINENCE	HEIGHT RANK	MV RATING	DATE CLIMBED
601	Mayo	37	L919₉₉ 643₃₈	26m	264	9.4	

CLASSIFICATION	MOUNTAIN NAME		ALTERNATIVE NAME				SUB-AREA
Ⓐ	**Bunnacunneen**		*Ir: Bun an Choinín, 'the end or tail of the rabbit'*				Joyce Country
HEIGHT METRES	COUNTY	1:50K MAP NO.	MAP GRID REF	PROMINENCE	HEIGHT RANK	MV RATING	DATE CLIMBED
575	Galway	38	L938₉₆ 577₃₄	463m	310	8.1	

CLASSIFICATION	MOUNTAIN NAME		ALTERNATIVE NAME				SUB-AREA
Ⓐ	**Ben Beg**		*Ir: Binn Bheag, 'little peak'*				Joyce Country
HEIGHT METRES	COUNTY	1:50K MAP NO.	MAP GRID REF	PROMINENCE	HEIGHT RANK	MV RATING	DATE CLIMBED
560	Galway	38	L950₉₃ 578₉₄	135m	335	7.9	

CLASSIFICATION	MOUNTAIN NAME		ALTERNATIVE NAME				SUB-AREA
Ⓐ	**Knocklaur**		*Ir: Cnoc Láir, 'middle hill'*				Partry Mtns
HEIGHT METRES	COUNTY	1:50K MAP NO.	MAP GRID REF	PROMINENCE	HEIGHT RANK	MV RATING	DATE CLIMBED
518	Mayo/Galway	38	L935₈₉ 630₉₀	43m	406	9.3	

CLASSIFICATION	MOUNTAIN NAME		ALTERNATIVE NAME				SUB-AREA
Ⓐ	**Barnahowna**		*Ir: Mám Cam, 'crooked pass'*				Partry Mtns
HEIGHT METRES	COUNTY	1:50K MAP NO.	MAP GRID REF	PROMINENCE	HEIGHT RANK	MV RATING	DATE CLIMBED
516	Mayo	38	M002₀₀ 675₀₀	71m	414	7.5	

Descending from Bunnacunneen to the col with Ben Beg

Purple Mountain summit with views to MacGillycuddy's Reeks

PURPLE MOUNTAIN

CLASSIFICATION	MOUNTAIN NAME		ALTERNATIVE NAME				SUB-AREA
Ⓐ ⓋⓁ	**Purple Mtn**		*Ir: An Sliabh Corcra, 'purple mountain'*				
HEIGHT METRES	COUNTY	1:50K MAP NO.	MAP GRID REF	PROMINENCE	HEIGHT RANK	MV RATING	DATE CLIMBED
832	Kerry	78	V886₄₀ 851₇₂	597m	27	9.0	

CLASSIFICATION	MOUNTAIN NAME		ALTERNATIVE NAME				SUB-AREA
Ⓐ ⓋⓁ	**Shehy Mtn**		*Ir: Seiche, 'a hide or skin'*				
HEIGHT METRES	COUNTY	1:50K MAP NO.	MAP GRID REF	PROMINENCE	HEIGHT RANK	MV RATING	DATE CLIMBED
762	Kerry	78	V901₇₉ 857₀₆	47m	67	8.6	

CLASSIFICATION	MOUNTAIN NAME		ALTERNATIVE NAME				SUB-AREA
ⓋⓁ	**Purple Mtn NE Top**		*Ir: An Sliabh Corcra, 'purple mountain'*				
HEIGHT METRES	COUNTY	1:50K MAP NO.	MAP GRID REF	PROMINENCE	HEIGHT RANK	MV RATING	DATE CLIMBED
757	Kerry	78	V894₃₅ 858₄₁	35m	71	8.1	

CLASSIFICATION	MOUNTAIN NAME		ALTERNATIVE NAME				SUB-AREA
Ⓐ ⓋⓁ	**Tomies Mtn**		*Ir: An Chathair, 'stone fort'*				
HEIGHT METRES	COUNTY	1:50K MAP NO.	MAP GRID REF	PROMINENCE	HEIGHT RANK	MV RATING	DATE CLIMBED
735	Kerry	78	V894₉₉ 867₆₇	60m	83	8.3	

SHANNON

CLASSIFICATION	MOUNTAIN NAME		ALTERNATIVE NAME				SUB-AREA
Ⓐ Ⓥ	**Keeper Hill**		*Ir: Sliabh Coimeálta, 'mountain of guarding'*				Keeper Hill
HEIGHT METRES	COUNTY	1:50K MAP NO.	MAP GRID REF	PROMINENCE	HEIGHT RANK	MV RATING	DATE CLIMBED
694	Tipperary	59	R823₉₇ 666₉₇	627m	115	6.4	

CLASSIFICATION	MOUNTAIN NAME		ALTERNATIVE NAME				SUB-AREA
Ⓐ	**Mauherslieve**		*Mother Mountain. Ir: Motharshliabh, 'wilderness mtn'*				Mauherslieve
HEIGHT METRES	COUNTY	1:50K MAP NO.	MAP GRID REF	PROMINENCE	HEIGHT RANK	MV RATING	DATE CLIMBED
543	Tipperary	59	R873₂₃ 619₃₈	268m	360	7.2	

CLASSIFICATION	MOUNTAIN NAME		ALTERNATIVE NAME				SUB-AREA
Ⓐ	**Moylussa**						Slieve Bernagh
HEIGHT METRES	COUNTY	1:50K MAP NO.	MAP GRID REF	PROMINENCE	HEIGHT RANK	MV RATING	DATE CLIMBED
531.6*	Clare	58	R648₄₄ 759₂₈	502m	382	6.2	

CLASSIFICATION	MOUNTAIN NAME		ALTERNATIVE NAME				SUB-AREA
Ⓐ	**Cragnamurragh**						Slieve Bernagh
HEIGHT METRES	COUNTY	1:50K MAP NO.	MAP GRID REF	PROMINENCE	HEIGHT RANK	MV RATING	DATE CLIMBED
526	Clare	58	R628₈₁ 749₅₀	51m	393	5.9	

Mauherslieve summit, Keeper Hill in the distance

Looking east from Barrclashcame along the Sheefrys Ridge towards Tievummera

SHEEFRY HILLS

CLASSIFICATION	MOUNTAIN NAME	ALTERNATIVE NAME					SUB-AREA
Ⓐ Ⓥ	**Barraclashcame**	*Ir: Barr Chlais Céim, top of the trench of the step'*					
HEIGHT METRES	COUNTY	1:50K MAP NO.	MAP GRID REF	PROMINENCE	HEIGHT RANK	MV RATING	DATE CLIMBED
772	Mayo	37	L849₅₁ 695₁₅	707m	59	8.8	

CLASSIFICATION	MOUNTAIN NAME	ALTERNATIVE NAME					SUB-AREA
Ⓐ Ⓥ	**Tievummera**	*Ir: Taobh Iomaire, 'side of the ridge'*					
HEIGHT METRES	COUNTY	1:50K MAP NO.	MAP GRID REF	PROMINENCE	HEIGHT RANK	MV RATING	DATE CLIMBED
762	Mayo	37	L861₃₉ 694₅₂	37m	66	9.1	

CLASSIFICATION	MOUNTAIN NAME	ALTERNATIVE NAME					SUB-AREA
Ⓐ Ⓥ	**Tievnabinnia**	*Ir: Taobh na Binne, 'side of the peak'*					
HEIGHT METRES	COUNTY	1:50K MAP NO.	MAP GRID REF	PROMINENCE	HEIGHT RANK	MV RATING	DATE CLIMBED
742	Mayo	37	L880₉₂ 706₅₄	37m	81	8.6	

CLASSIFICATION	MOUNTAIN NAME	ALTERNATIVE NAME					SUB-AREA
Ⓐ	**Tievnabinnia E Top**	*Ir: Taobh na Binne, 'side of the peak'*					
HEIGHT METRES	COUNTY	1:50K MAP NO.	MAP GRID REF	PROMINENCE	HEIGHT RANK	MV RATING	DATE CLIMBED
590	Mayo	37	L897₄₁ 705₉₅	55m	287	9.0	

CLASSIFICATION	MOUNTAIN NAME	ALTERNATIVE NAME		SUB-AREA
Ⓐ	**Barraclashcame NW Top**	*Ir: Starraicín na gCaor, 'pinnacle of the berries'*		

HEIGHT METRES	COUNTY	1:50K MAP NO.	MAP GRID REF	PROMINENCE	HEIGHT RANK	MV RATING	DATE CLIMBED
580	Mayo	37	L849$_{51}$ 695$_{15}$	45m	303	8.0	

CLASSIFICATION	MOUNTAIN NAME	ALTERNATIVE NAME		SUB-AREA
Ⓐ	**Tawny Rower**			

HEIGHT METRES	COUNTY	1:50K MAP NO.	MAP GRID REF	PROMINENCE	HEIGHT RANK	MV RATING	DATE CLIMBED
510	Mayo	37	L918$_{91}$ 713$_{93}$	95m	425	8.1	

SHEHY/KNOCKBOY

CLASSIFICATION	MOUNTAIN NAME	ALTERNATIVE NAME		SUB-AREA
Ⓐ Ⓥⓛ	**Knockboy**	*Ir: An Cnoc Buí, 'yellow/golden hill'*		

HEIGHT METRES	COUNTY	1:50K MAP NO.	MAP GRID REF	PROMINENCE	HEIGHT RANK	MV RATING	DATE CLIMBED
706	Cork/Kerry	85	W004$_{80}$ 620$_{60}$	685m	103	8.2	

CLASSIFICATION	MOUNTAIN NAME	ALTERNATIVE NAME		SUB-AREA
Ⓐ Ⓥⓛ	**Caoinkeen**	*Ir: An Caincín, 'snub nose or turned-up nose'*		

HEIGHT METRES	COUNTY	1:50K MAP NO.	MAP GRID REF	PROMINENCE	HEIGHT RANK	MV RATING	DATE CLIMBED
692	Cork/Kerry	85	W010$_{40}$ 645$_{57}$	107m	118	9.0	

CLASSIFICATION	MOUNTAIN NAME	ALTERNATIVE NAME		SUB-AREA
Ⓐ Ⓥⓛ	**Knocknamanagh**	*Ir: Cnoc na Manach, 'hill of the monks'*		

HEIGHT METRES	COUNTY	1:50K MAP NO.	MAP GRID REF	PROMINENCE	HEIGHT RANK	MV RATING	DATE CLIMBED
637	Kerry	85	V990$_{61}$ 661$_{30}$	139m	212	7.7	

CLASSIFICATION	MOUNTAIN NAME	ALTERNATIVE NAME		SUB-AREA
Ⓐ Ⓥⓛ	**Knocknamanagh NE Top**	*Ir: Cnoc na Manach, 'hill of the monks'*		

HEIGHT METRES	COUNTY	1:50K MAP NO.	MAP GRID REF	PROMINENCE	HEIGHT RANK	MV RATING	DATE CLIMBED
625	Kerry	85	W001$_{85}$ 672$_{29}$	60m	231	7.1	

CLASSIFICATION	MOUNTAIN NAME	ALTERNATIVE NAME		SUB-AREA
Ⓐ Ⓥⓛ	**Carran**	*Ir: An Carn, 'the cairn'*		

HEIGHT METRES	COUNTY	1:50K MAP NO.	MAP GRID REF	PROMINENCE	HEIGHT RANK	MV RATING	DATE CLIMBED
604	Kerry	85	W052$_{51}$ 678$_{91}$	237m	255	6.8	

CLASSIFICATION	MOUNTAIN NAME	ALTERNATIVE NAME		SUB-AREA
Ⓐ Ⓥⓛ	**Gullaba Hill**	*Ir: Cnoc Ghullaba, 'hill of the beak/snout'*		

HEIGHT METRES	COUNTY	1:50K MAP NO.	MAP GRID REF	PROMINENCE	HEIGHT RANK	MV RATING	DATE CLIMBED
603	Kerry	85	W005$_{08}$ 681$_{82}$	38m	258	8.3	

CLASSIFICATION	MOUNTAIN NAME	ALTERNATIVE NAME		SUB-AREA
Ⓐ	**Carran S Top**	*Ir: An Carn, 'the cairn'*		

HEIGHT METRES	COUNTY	1:50K MAP NO.	MAP GRID REF	PROMINENCE	HEIGHT RANK	MV RATING	DATE CLIMBED
567	Kerry	85	W054$_{68}$ 670$_{36}$	42m	324	6.4	

Dark clouds gather over Caoinkeen's summit

CLASSIFICATION	MOUNTAIN NAME		ALTERNATIVE NAME			SUB-AREA	
A	**Conigar**		Ir: An Coinigéar, 'the warren'				
HEIGHT METRES	COUNTY	1:50K MAP NO.	MAP GRID REF	PROMINENCE	HEIGHT RANK	MV RATING	DATE CLIMBED
566	Cork	85	W066₃₆ 638₇₄	131m	326	5.7	

CLASSIFICATION	MOUNTAIN NAME		ALTERNATIVE NAME			SUB-AREA	
A	**Carran NE Top**		Ir: An Carn, 'the cairn'				
HEIGHT METRES	COUNTY	1:50K MAP NO.	MAP GRID REF	PROMINENCE	HEIGHT RANK	MV RATING	DATE CLIMBED
561	Kerry	85	W066₄₂ 694₁₃	36m	333	6.4	

CLASSIFICATION	MOUNTAIN NAME		ALTERNATIVE NAME			SUB-AREA	
A	**Shehy More**		Ir: An tSeithe Mhór, poss. 'the big hide'				
HEIGHT METRES	COUNTY	1:50K MAP NO.	MAP GRID REF	PROMINENCE	HEIGHT RANK	MV RATING	DATE CLIMBED
546	Cork	85	W152₀₀ 600₀₀	351m	357	6.4	

CLASSIFICATION	MOUNTAIN NAME		ALTERNATIVE NAME			SUB-AREA	
A	**Nowen Hill**		Ir: Cnoc na nAbhann, 'hill of the rivers'				
HEIGHT METRES	COUNTY	1:50K MAP NO.	MAP GRID REF	PROMINENCE	HEIGHT RANK	MV RATING	DATE CLIMBED
535.2*	Cork	85	W140₆₇ 529₀₁	300m	376	7.3	

CLASSIFICATION	MOUNTAIN NAME		ALTERNATIVE NAME			SUB-AREA	
A	**Knockboy S Top**		Ir: An Cnoc Buí, 'yellow/golden hill'				
HEIGHT METRES	COUNTY	1:50K MAP NO.	MAP GRID REF	PROMINENCE	HEIGHT RANK	MV RATING	DATE CLIMBED
532	Cork	85	W006₀₀ 605₀₀	37m	381	5.4	

CLASSIFICATION	MOUNTAIN NAME		ALTERNATIVE NAME				SUB-AREA
Ⓐ	**Coomataggart**		*Ir:Com an tSagairt, 'hollow of the priest'*				
HEIGHT METRES	COUNTY	1:50K MAP NO.	MAP GRID REF	PROMINENCE	HEIGHT RANK	MV RATING	DATE CLIMBED
530	Cork/Kerry	85	W101$_{16}$ 688$_{80}$	75m	387	7.9	

CLASSIFICATION	MOUNTAIN NAME		ALTERNATIVE NAME				SUB-AREA
Ⓐ	**The Priests Leap**		*Cummeenshrule. Ir: Léim an tSagairt, 'the priest's leap'*				
HEIGHT METRES	COUNTY	1:50K MAP NO.	MAP GRID REF	PROMINENCE	HEIGHT RANK	MV RATING	DATE CLIMBED
519	Cork/Kerry	85	V978$_{26}$ 606$_{47}$	54m	405	6.5	

CLASSIFICATION	MOUNTAIN NAME		ALTERNATIVE NAME				SUB-AREA
Ⓐ	**Nowen Hill SW Top**		*Derreenacrinnig E. Ir: Cnoc na nAbhann, 'hill of the rivers'*				
HEIGHT METRES	COUNTY	1:50K MAP NO.	MAP GRID REF	PROMINENCE	HEIGHT RANK	MV RATING	DATE CLIMBED
509	Cork	85	W128$_{00}$ 520$_{54}$	44m	430	5.9	

CLASSIFICATION	MOUNTAIN NAME		ALTERNATIVE NAME				SUB-AREA
Ⓐ	**Carran Far N Top**		*Ir: An Carn, 'the cairn'*				
HEIGHT METRES	COUNTY	1:50K MAP NO.	MAP GRID REF	PROMINENCE	HEIGHT RANK	MV RATING	DATE CLIMBED
506	Kerry	79	W055$_{84}$ 701$_{49}$	41m	436	5.2	

A rainbow over the Carran group, seen from the minor summit of Bird Hill

Stone beacon on the Ridge of Capard in the Slieve Bloom Mountains

SLIEVE BLOOM

CLASSIFICATION	MOUNTAIN NAME		ALTERNATIVE NAME				SUB-AREA
Ⓐ	**Arderin**		*Ir: Ard Éireann, 'the height of Ireland' or 'Eriu's height'*				
HEIGHT METRES	COUNTY	1:50K MAP NO.	MAP GRID REF	PROMINENCE	HEIGHT RANK	MV RATING	DATE CLIMBED
527	Laois/Offaly	54	S232₄₈ 989₀₄	420m	391	5.3	

CLASSIFICATION	MOUNTAIN NAME		ALTERNATIVE NAME				SUB-AREA
Ⓐ	**Stillbrook Hill**						
HEIGHT METRES	COUNTY	1:50K MAP NO.	MAP GRID REF	PROMINENCE	HEIGHT RANK	MV RATING	DATE CLIMBED
514	Offaly	54	N261₄₉ 029₇₉	79m	419	5.3	

CLASSIFICATION	MOUNTAIN NAME		ALTERNATIVE NAME				SUB-AREA
Ⓐ	**Baunreaghcong**						
HEIGHT METRES	COUNTY	1:50K MAP NO.	MAP GRID REF	PROMINENCE	HEIGHT RANK	MV RATING	DATE CLIMBED
509	Laois	54	N325₈₅ 036₅₇	74m	431	5.4	

SLIEVE MISH

CLASSIFICATION	MOUNTAIN NAME	ALTERNATIVE NAME				SUB-AREA
A **VL**	**Baurtregaum**	*Ir: Barr Trí gCom, 'top of three hollows'*				
HEIGHT METRES	COUNTY	1:50K MAP NO.	MAP GRID REF	PROMINENCE	HEIGHT RANK	MV RATING	DATE CLIMBED
851	Kerry	71	Q749₈₆ 076₆₇	643m	17	8.4

CLASSIFICATION	MOUNTAIN NAME	ALTERNATIVE NAME				SUB-AREA
A **VL**	**Caherconree**	*Ir: Cathair Conraoi, 'Cú Roí's stone fort'*				
HEIGHT METRES	COUNTY	1:50K MAP NO.	MAP GRID REF	PROMINENCE	HEIGHT RANK	MV RATING	DATE CLIMBED
835	Kerry	71	Q733₁₈ 072₆₀	129m	26	8.7

CLASSIFICATION	MOUNTAIN NAME	ALTERNATIVE NAME				SUB-AREA
VL	**Gearhane**	*Ir: An Géarán, 'the fang'*				
HEIGHT METRES	COUNTY	1:50K MAP NO.	MAP GRID REF	PROMINENCE	HEIGHT RANK	MV RATING	DATE CLIMBED
792	Kerry	71	Q733₂₂ 082₉₃	17m	46	8.9

CLASSIFICATION	MOUNTAIN NAME	ALTERNATIVE NAME				SUB-AREA
VL	**Baurtregaum NW Top**	*Ir: Barr Trí gCom, 'top of three hollows'*				
HEIGHT METRES	COUNTY	1:50K MAP NO.	MAP GRID REF	PROMINENCE	HEIGHT RANK	MV RATING	DATE CLIMBED
723	Kerry	71	Q747₂₄ 083₅₇	18m	92	9.3

CLASSIFICATION	MOUNTAIN NAME	ALTERNATIVE NAME				SUB-AREA
VL	**Baurtregaum Far NE Top**	*Ir: Barr Trí gCom, 'top of three hollows'*				
HEIGHT METRES	COUNTY	1:50K MAP NO.	MAP GRID REF	PROMINENCE	HEIGHT RANK	MV RATING	DATE CLIMBED
603	Kerry	71	Q768₆₆ 090₅₄	28m	256	8.2

Caherconree from Caherbla

Looking south-west over Dingle Bay from Baurtregaum

CLASSIFICATION	MOUNTAIN NAME		ALTERNATIVE NAME			SUB-AREA	
Ⓐ Ⓥ	**Castle Hill**						

HEIGHT METRES	COUNTY	1:50K MAP NO.	MAP GRID REF	PROMINENCE	HEIGHT RANK	MV RATING	DATE CLIMBED
600	Kerry	71	Q756₂₂ 063₅₇	35m	267	8.6	

CLASSIFICATION	MOUNTAIN NAME		ALTERNATIVE NAME			SUB-AREA	
Ⓐ	**Caherbla**		*Ballyarkane Oughter .Ir: Cathair Bhláth, 'stone fort of flowers'*				

HEIGHT METRES	COUNTY	1:50K MAP NO.	MAP GRID REF	PROMINENCE	HEIGHT RANK	MV RATING	DATE CLIMBED
586	Kerry	71	Q724₀₅ 051₁₈	91m	293	7.6	

CLASSIFICATION	MOUNTAIN NAME		ALTERNATIVE NAME			SUB-AREA	
Ⓐ	**Moanlaur**		*Ir: Móin Láir, 'middle bog'*				

HEIGHT METRES	COUNTY	1:50K MAP NO.	MAP GRID REF	PROMINENCE	HEIGHT RANK	MV RATING	DATE CLIMBED
566	Kerry	71	Q689₆₄ 044₆₀	289m	325	7.7	

CLASSIFICATION	MOUNTAIN NAME		ALTERNATIVE NAME			SUB-AREA	
Ⓐ	**Barnanageehy**		*Ir: Bearna na Gaoithe, 'gap of the wind'*				

HEIGHT METRES	COUNTY	1:50K MAP NO.	MAP GRID REF	PROMINENCE	HEIGHT RANK	MV RATING	DATE CLIMBED
561	Kerry	71	Q800₄₅ 082₅₃	56m	332	7.2	

CLASSIFICATION	MOUNTAIN NAME		ALTERNATIVE NAME			SUB-AREA	
Ⓐ	**Beenduff**		*Ir: An Bhinn Dubh, 'the black peak'*				

HEIGHT METRES	COUNTY	1:50K MAP NO.	MAP GRID REF	PROMINENCE	HEIGHT RANK	MV RATING	DATE CLIMBED
515	Kerry	71	Q676₉₇ 036₅₈	40m	415	7.4	

Slievenamon summit cairn

SOUTH MIDLANDS

CLASSIFICATION	MOUNTAIN NAME	ALTERNATIVE NAME				SUB-AREA
Ⓐ Ⓥ	**Slievenamon**	*Ir: Sliabh na mBan, 'mountain of the women'*				
HEIGHT METRES	**COUNTY**	**1:50K MAP NO.**	**MAP GRID REF**	**PROMINENCE**	**HEIGHT RANK**	**MV RATING**	**DATE CLIMBED**
721	Tipperary	67	S297₈₂ 307₂₂ 711m	94	6.6	

CLASSIFICATION	MOUNTAIN NAME	ALTERNATIVE NAME				SUB-AREA
Ⓐ	**Brandon Hill**	*Ir: Cnoc Bhréanail, 'hill of Bréanal'*				
HEIGHT METRES	**COUNTY**	**1:50K MAP NO.**	**MAP GRID REF**	**PROMINENCE**	**HEIGHT RANK**	**MV RATING**	**DATE CLIMBED**
515	Kilkenny	68	S697₀₂ 402₆₇ 450m	416	6.3	

CLASSIFICATION	MOUNTAIN NAME	ALTERNATIVE NAME				SUB-AREA
Ⓐ	**Knockahunna**	*Ir: Cnoc an Chonnaidh, 'hill of the firewood'*				
HEIGHT METRES	**COUNTY**	**1:50K MAP NO.**	**MAP GRID REF**	**PROMINENCE**	**HEIGHT RANK**	**MV RATING**	**DATE CLIMBED**
502	Tipperary	67	S303₁₁ 327₅₄ 47m	446	5.7	

SPERRIN MOUNTAINS

CLASSIFICATION	MOUNTAIN NAME	ALTERNATIVE NAME				SUB-AREA
Ⓐ Ⓥ	**Sawel**	*Ir: 'Samhail Phite Méabha,' 'resemblance of Maeve's vulva'*				
HEIGHT METRES	**COUNTY**	**1:50K MAP NO.**	**MAP GRID REF**	**PROMINENCE**	**HEIGHT RANK**	**MV RATING**	**DATE CLIMBED**
678	Derry/Tyrone	13	H617₉₆ 973₀₅ 657m	140	8.3	

CLASSIFICATION	MOUNTAIN NAME	ALTERNATIVE NAME				SUB-AREA
Ⓐ Ⓥ	**Mullaghclogha**	*Ir: Mullach Clocha, 'summit of stones'*				
HEIGHT METRES	**COUNTY**	**1:50K MAP NO.**	**MAP GRID REF**	**PROMINENCE**	**HEIGHT RANK**	**MV RATING**	**DATE CLIMBED**
635	Tyrone	13	H556₀₀ 958₀₀ 207m	217	7.1	

CLASSIFICATION	MOUNTAIN NAME		ALTERNATIVE NAME				SUB-AREA
(A) (VL)	**Mullaghaneany**		*Ir: Mullach an Ionaidh, 'summit of the wonder'*				
HEIGHT METRES	COUNTY	1:50K MAP NO.	MAP GRID REF	PROMINENCE	HEIGHT RANK	MV RATING	DATE CLIMBED
627	Derry/Tyrone	13	H685₄₀ 986₂₃	302m	228	8.3	

CLASSIFICATION	MOUNTAIN NAME		ALTERNATIVE NAME				SUB-AREA
(A) (VL)	**Meenard Mtn**		*Ir: Mín Ard, 'high mountain pasture'*				
HEIGHT METRES	COUNTY	1:50K MAP NO.	MAP GRID REF	PROMINENCE	HEIGHT RANK	MV RATING	DATE CLIMBED
620	Derry/Tyrone	13	H672₉₂ 985₆₅	85m	237	8.6	

CLASSIFICATION	MOUNTAIN NAME		ALTERNATIVE NAME				SUB-AREA
(A) (VL)	**Dart Mtn**		*Ir: An Dairt, 'the lump'*				
HEIGHT METRES	COUNTY	1:50K MAP NO.	MAP GRID REF	PROMINENCE	HEIGHT RANK	MV RATING	DATE CLIMBED
619	Derry/Tyrone	13	H602₅₄ 963₀₉	89m	238	7.5	

CLASSIFICATION	MOUNTAIN NAME		ALTERNATIVE NAME				SUB-AREA
(A)	**Mullaghasturrakeen**		*Ir: Mullach an Starracín, 'summit of the steeple'*				
HEIGHT METRES	COUNTY	1:50K MAP NO.	MAP GRID REF	PROMINENCE	HEIGHT RANK	MV RATING	DATE CLIMBED
581	Tyrone	13	H548₀₀ 950₀₀	46m	302	8.5	

CLASSIFICATION	MOUNTAIN NAME		ALTERNATIVE NAME				SUB-AREA
(A)	**Mullaghclogher**		*Ir: Mullach Clochair, 'summit of the stony patch'*				
HEIGHT METRES	COUNTY	1:50K MAP NO.	MAP GRID REF	PROMINENCE	HEIGHT RANK	MV RATING	DATE CLIMBED
572	Tyrone	13	H530₀₀ 949₀₀	127m	317	8.7	

CLASSIFICATION	MOUNTAIN NAME		ALTERNATIVE NAME				SUB-AREA
(A)	**Oughtmore**		*Ir: Ucht Mór, 'big mountain-breast'*				
HEIGHT METRES	COUNTY	1:50K MAP NO.	MAP GRID REF	PROMINENCE	HEIGHT RANK	MV RATING	DATE CLIMBED
569	Derry/Tyrone	13	H700₀₄ 974₉₂	104m	323	8.6	

CLASSIFICATION	MOUNTAIN NAME		ALTERNATIVE NAME				SUB-AREA
(A)	**Carnanelly**		*Ir: Carnán Aichle, 'little cairn of the lookout point'*				
HEIGHT METRES	COUNTY	1:50K MAP NO.	MAP GRID REF	PROMINENCE	HEIGHT RANK	MV RATING	DATE CLIMBED
562	Tyrone	13	H675₄₇ 921₂₇	307m	331	7.4	

CLASSIFICATION	MOUNTAIN NAME		ALTERNATIVE NAME				SUB-AREA
(A)	**Mullaghmore**		*Ir: Mullach Mór, 'big summit'*				
HEIGHT METRES	COUNTY	1:50K MAP NO.	MAP GRID REF	PROMINENCE	HEIGHT RANK	MV RATING	DATE CLIMBED
550	Derry	8	C738₅₈ 008₂₆	235m	351	6.4	

CLASSIFICATION	MOUNTAIN NAME		ALTERNATIVE NAME				SUB-AREA
(A)	**Mullaghcarn**		*Ir: Mullach Cairn, 'summit of the cairn'*				
HEIGHT METRES	COUNTY	1:50K MAP NO.	MAP GRID REF	PROMINENCE	HEIGHT RANK	MV RATING	DATE CLIMBED
542	Tyrone	13	H510₅₃ 809₇₆	377m	363	5.9	

Following the fence to Mullaghsturrakeen in the Sperrins

CLASSIFICATION	MOUNTAIN NAME		ALTERNATIVE NAME				SUB-AREA	
Ⓐ	**White Mtn**		*Ir: Sliabh Bán, 'white mountain'*					
HEIGHT METRES	COUNTY	1:50K MAP NO.	MAP GRID REF	PROMINENCE	HEIGHT RANK	MV RATING	DATE CLIMBED	
537	Derry	8	C741$_{27}$ 021$_{58}$	42m	372	6.6		

CLASSIFICATION	MOUNTAIN NAME		ALTERNATIVE NAME				SUB-AREA	
Ⓐ	**Slieve Gallion**		*Ir: Sliabh gCallann, 'mountain of the heights'*					
HEIGHT METRES	COUNTY	1:50K MAP NO.	MAP GRID REF	PROMINENCE	HEIGHT RANK	MV RATING	DATE CLIMBED	
528	Derry	13	H798$_{55}$ 878$_{03}$	333m	390	6.8		

CLASSIFICATION	MOUNTAIN NAME		ALTERNATIVE NAME				SUB-AREA	
Ⓐ	**Crockbrack**		*Ir: Cnoc Breac, 'speckled hill'*					
HEIGHT METRES	COUNTY	1:50K MAP NO.	MAP GRID REF	PROMINENCE	HEIGHT RANK	MV RATING	DATE CLIMBED	
526	Derry	13	H718$_{18}$ 957$_{82}$	151m	395	7.1		

CLASSIFICATION	MOUNTAIN NAME		ALTERNATIVE NAME				SUB-AREA	
Ⓐ	**Mullaghcarbatagh**		*Mullach Carbadach, 'boulder-strewn summit'*					
HEIGHT METRES	COUNTY	1:50K MAP NO.	MAP GRID REF	PROMINENCE	HEIGHT RANK	MV RATING	DATE CLIMBED	
517	Tyrone	13	H518$_{13}$ 947$_{86}$	32m	411	8.3		

CLASSIFICATION	MOUNTAIN NAME		ALTERNATIVE NAME				SUB-AREA	
Ⓐ	**Carnanelly W Top**		*Ir: Carnán Aichle, 'little cairn of the lookout point'*					
HEIGHT METRES	COUNTY	1:50K MAP NO.	MAP GRID REF	PROMINENCE	HEIGHT RANK	MV RATING	DATE CLIMBED	
505	Tyrone	13	H663$_{84}$ 920$_{95}$	30m	439	7.1		

Ascending Carnanelly from the east

The rugged prospect south from Benbreen to Bengower in the Twelve Bens

CLASSIFICATION	MOUNTAIN NAME	ALTERNATIVE NAME		SUB-AREA
A VL	**Benbaun**	Ir: Binn Bhán, 'white peak'		

HEIGHT METRES	COUNTY	1:50K MAP NO.	MAP GRID REF	PROMINENCE	HEIGHT RANK	MV RATING	DATE CLIMBED
729	Galway	37	L785$_{58}$ 539$_{03}$	684m	88	8.9	

CLASSIFICATION	MOUNTAIN NAME	ALTERNATIVE NAME		SUB-AREA
A VL	**Bencorr**	Ir: Binn Chorr, 'pointed peak'		

HEIGHT METRES	COUNTY	1:50K MAP NO.	MAP GRID REF	PROMINENCE	HEIGHT RANK	MV RATING	DATE CLIMBED
711	Galway	37	L811$_{66}$ 522$_{00}$	306m	100	9.5	

CLASSIFICATION	MOUNTAIN NAME	ALTERNATIVE NAME		SUB-AREA
A VL	**Bencollaghduff**	Ir: Binn Dubh, 'black peak'		

HEIGHT METRES	COUNTY	1:50K MAP NO.	MAP GRID REF	PROMINENCE	HEIGHT RANK	MV RATING	DATE CLIMBED
696	Galway	37	L797$_{80}$ 529$_{93}$	191m	113	9.7	

CLASSIFICATION	MOUNTAIN NAME	ALTERNATIVE NAME		SUB-AREA
A VL	**Benbreen**	Ir: Binn Bhraoin, 'Braon's peak'		

HEIGHT METRES	COUNTY	1:50K MAP NO.	MAP GRID REF	PROMINENCE	HEIGHT RANK	MV RATING	DATE CLIMBED
691	Galway	37	L783$_{11}$ 515$_{47}$	186m	120	9.4	

CLASSIFICATION	MOUNTAIN NAME	ALTERNATIVE NAME		SUB-AREA
VL	**Benbreen Central Top**	Ir: Binn Bhraoin, 'Braon's peak'		

HEIGHT METRES	COUNTY	1:50K MAP NO.	MAP GRID REF	PROMINENCE	HEIGHT RANK	MV RATING	DATE CLIMBED
680	Galway	37	L781$_{04}$ 519$_{97}$	25m	134	9.6	

CLASSIFICATION	MOUNTAIN NAME	ALTERNATIVE NAME		SUB-AREA
A VL	**Derryclare**	Ir: Binn Doire Chláir, 'peak of Derryclare'		

HEIGHT METRES	COUNTY	1:50K MAP NO.	MAP GRID REF	PROMINENCE	HEIGHT RANK	MV RATING	DATE CLIMBED
677	Galway	37	L815$_{09}$ 510$_{48}$	129m	142	8.8	

CLASSIFICATION	MOUNTAIN NAME	ALTERNATIVE NAME		SUB-AREA
VL	**Benbreen North Top**	Ir: Binn Bhraoin, 'Braon's peak'		

HEIGHT METRES	COUNTY	1:50K MAP NO.	MAP GRID REF	PROMINENCE	HEIGHT RANK	MV RATING	DATE CLIMBED
674	Galway	37	L784$_{35}$ 521$_{85}$	16m	145	9.5	

CLASSIFICATION	MOUNTAIN NAME	ALTERNATIVE NAME		SUB-AREA
A VL	**Bengower**	Ir: Binn Gabhar, 'goat's peak'		

HEIGHT METRES	COUNTY	1:50K MAP NO.	MAP GRID REF	PROMINENCE	HEIGHT RANK	MV RATING	DATE CLIMBED
664	Galway	37	L783$_{01}$ 506$_{44}$	196m	163	8.9	

CLASSIFICATION	MOUNTAIN NAME	ALTERNATIVE NAME		SUB-AREA
A VL	**Muckanaght**	Ir: Meacanacht, 'hill like a pig's back'		

HEIGHT METRES	COUNTY	1:50K MAP NO.	MAP GRID REF	PROMINENCE	HEIGHT RANK	MV RATING	DATE CLIMBED
654	Galway	37	L767$_{83}$ 540$_{83}$	179m	178	8.9	

Bencollaghduff and Benbaun from Gleninagh

CLASSIFICATION	MOUNTAIN NAME		ALTERNATIVE NAME				SUB-AREA
Ⓐ Ⓥ	**Benfree**		*Ir: Binn Fraoigh, 'peak of heather'*				
HEIGHT METRES	COUNTY	1:50K MAP NO.	MAP GRID REF	PROMINENCE	HEIGHT RANK	MV RATING	DATE CLIMBED
638	Galway	37	L777$_{58}$ 544$_{12}$	48m	210	8.4	

CLASSIFICATION	MOUNTAIN NAME		ALTERNATIVE NAME				SUB-AREA
Ⓐ Ⓥ	**Bencullagh**		*Ir: An Chailleach, 'the hag'*				
HEIGHT METRES	COUNTY	1:50K MAP NO.	MAP GRID REF	PROMINENCE	HEIGHT RANK	MV RATING	DATE CLIMBED
632	Galway	37	L755$_{77}$ 537$_{24}$	154m	220	8.9	

CLASSIFICATION	MOUNTAIN NAME		ALTERNATIVE NAME				SUB-AREA
Ⓐ Ⓥ	**Maumonght**		*Ir: Mám Uchta, 'pass of the breast/ridge'*				
HEIGHT METRES	COUNTY	1:50K MAP NO.	MAP GRID REF	PROMINENCE	HEIGHT RANK	MV RATING	DATE CLIMBED
602	Galway	37	L749$_{49}$ 539$_{16}$	54m	262	7.7	

CLASSIFICATION	MOUNTAIN NAME		ALTERNATIVE NAME				SUB-AREA
Ⓐ	**Garraun**		*Ir: Maolchnoc, 'bald hill'*				
HEIGHT METRES	COUNTY	1:50K MAP NO.	MAP GRID REF	PROMINENCE	HEIGHT RANK	MV RATING	DATE CLIMBED
598	Galway	37	L767$_{13}$ 610$_{36}$	553m	272	8.3	

CLASSIFICATION	MOUNTAIN NAME		ALTERNATIVE NAME				SUB-AREA
Ⓐ	**Benbrack**		*Ir: Binn Bhreac, 'speckled peak'*				
HEIGHT METRES	COUNTY	1:50K MAP NO.	MAP GRID REF	PROMINENCE	HEIGHT RANK	MV RATING	DATE CLIMBED
582	Galway	37	L765$_{58}$ 558$_{18}$	264m	299	8.6	

CLASSIFICATION	MOUNTAIN NAME		ALTERNATIVE NAME				SUB-AREA
Ⓐ	**Benchoona**		*Ir: Binn Chuanna, 'peak of Cuanna'*				
HEIGHT METRES	COUNTY	1:50K MAP NO.	MAP GRID REF	PROMINENCE	HEIGHT RANK	MV RATING	DATE CLIMBED
581	Galway	37	L763$_{12}$ 616$_{73}$	36m	301	8.8	

CLASSIFICATION	MOUNTAIN NAME		ALTERNATIVE NAME				SUB-AREA
A	**Benlettery**		*Ir: Binn Leitrí, 'peak of the wet hillsides'*				
HEIGHT METRES	COUNTY	1:50K MAP NO.	MAP GRID REF	PROMINENCE	HEIGHT RANK	MV RATING	DATE CLIMBED
577	Galway	44	L775₄₆ 495₃₇	62m	306	7.5	

CLASSIFICATION	MOUNTAIN NAME		ALTERNATIVE NAME				SUB-AREA
A	**Bencorrbeg**		*Ir: Binn an Choire Bhig, 'peak of the little corrie'*				
HEIGHT METRES	COUNTY	1:50K MAP NO.	MAP GRID REF	PROMINENCE	HEIGHT RANK	MV RATING	DATE CLIMBED
577	Galway	37	L816₅₀ 532₉₉	42m	307	8.8	

CLASSIFICATION	MOUNTAIN NAME		ALTERNATIVE NAME				SUB-AREA
A	**Garraun South Top**		*Ir: Maolchnoc, 'bald hill'*				
HEIGHT METRES	COUNTY	1:50K MAP NO.	MAP GRID REF	PROMINENCE	HEIGHT RANK	MV RATING	DATE CLIMBED
556	Galway	37	L763₃₂ 605₇₀	31m	340	7.7	

CLASSIFICATION	MOUNTAIN NAME		ALTERNATIVE NAME				SUB-AREA
A	**Doughruagh**		*Ir: Dúchruach, 'black stack'*				
HEIGHT METRES	COUNTY	1:50K MAP NO.	MAP GRID REF	PROMINENCE	HEIGHT RANK	MV RATING	DATE CLIMBED
526	Galway	37	L750₅₉ 594₃₀	211m	392	8.4	

CLASSIFICATION	MOUNTAIN NAME		ALTERNATIVE NAME				SUB-AREA
A	**Benglenisky**		*Ir: Binn Ghleann Uisce, 'peak of the glen of water'*				
HEIGHT METRES	COUNTY	1:50K MAP NO.	MAP GRID REF	PROMINENCE	HEIGHT RANK	MV RATING	DATE CLIMBED
516	Galway	44	L766₂₀ 500₆₄	48m	413	7.4	

Kylemore Lough from the summit of Doughruagh

THE COUNTY HIGHPOINTS

CLASSIFICATION	MOUNTAIN NAME	ALTERNATIVE NAME	AREA
(A) (VL)	**Carrauntoohil**	Ir: Corrán Tuathail, 'Tuathal's sickle'	M'GillyCuddy's R

HEIGHT METRES	COUNTY	1:50K MAP NO.	MAP GRID REF	PROMINENCE	COUNTY RANK	MV RATING	DATE CLIMBED
1,038.6*	Kerry	78	V803₆₃ 844₂₁	1,039m	1	8.3	

CLASSIFICATION	MOUNTAIN NAME	ALTERNATIVE NAME	AREA
(A) (VL)	**Lugnaquillia**	Ir: Log na Coille, 'hollow of the wood'	Wicklow Mtns

HEIGHT METRES	COUNTY	1:50K MAP NO.	MAP GRID REF	PROMINENCE	COUNTY RANK	MV RATING	DATE CLIMBED
925	Wicklow	56	T032₁₇ 917₅₆	905m	2	7.3	

CLASSIFICATION	MOUNTAIN NAME	ALTERNATIVE NAME	AREA
(A) (VL)	**Galtymore**	Ir: Cnoc Mór na nGaibhlte, 'big hill of the Galtees'	Galty Mtns

HEIGHT METRES	COUNTY	1:50K MAP NO.	MAP GRID REF	PROMINENCE	COUNTY RANK	MV RATING	DATE CLIMBED
917.9*	Limerick/Tipperary	74	R878₄₆ 237₈₈	898m	3	7.9	

CLASSIFICATION	MOUNTAIN NAME	ALTERNATIVE NAME	AREA
(A) (VL)	**Slieve Donard**	Ir: Sliabh Dónairt, 'mountain of (St) Domhangart'	Mourne Mtns

HEIGHT METRES	COUNTY	1:50K MAP NO.	MAP GRID REF	PROMINENCE	COUNTY RANK	MV RATING	DATE CLIMBED
850	Down	29	J357₉₆ 276₉₀	822m	4	7.7	

CLASSIFICATION	MOUNTAIN NAME	ALTERNATIVE NAME	AREA
(A) (VL)	**Mweelrea**	Ir: Cnoc Maol Réidh, 'bald hill with the smooth top'	Mweelrea Mtns

HEIGHT METRES	COUNTY	1:50K MAP NO.	MAP GRID REF	PROMINENCE	COUNTY RANK	MV RATING	DATE CLIMBED
814	Mayo	37	L789₈₃ 668₁₀	779m	5	9.2	

CLASSIFICATION	MOUNTAIN NAME	ALTERNATIVE NAME	AREA
(A) (VL)	**Mount Leinster**	Ir: Stua Laighean, 'prince (or warrior) of Leinster'	Blackstairs Mtns

HEIGHT METRES	COUNTY	1:50K MAP NO.	MAP GRID REF	PROMINENCE	COUNTY RANK	MV RATING	DATE CLIMBED
795	Carlow/Wexford	68	S826₀₃ 526₀₈	707m	6	7.8	

CLASSIFICATION	MOUNTAIN NAME	ALTERNATIVE NAME	AREA
(A) (VL)	**Knockmealdown**	Ir: Cnoc Mhaoldomhnaigh, 'hill of Maoldomhnach'	Knockmealdowns

HEIGHT METRES	COUNTY	1:50K MAP NO.	MAP GRID REF	PROMINENCE	COUNTY RANK	MV RATING	DATE CLIMBED
794	Tipperary/Waterford	74	S057₉₇ 084₁₀	682m	7	7.8	

CLASSIFICATION	MOUNTAIN NAME	ALTERNATIVE NAME	AREA
(A) (VL)	**Kippure**	Ir: Cipiúr, origin obscure	Dublin Mtns

HEIGHT METRES	COUNTY	1:50K MAP NO.	MAP GRID REF	PROMINENCE	COUNTY RANK	MV RATING	DATE CLIMBED
757	Dublin/Wicklow	56	O115₈₂ 154₅₅	262m	8	5.7	

CLASSIFICATION	MOUNTAIN NAME	ALTERNATIVE NAME	AREA
(A) (VL)	**Errigal**	Ir: An Earagail, poss. 'oratory'	Derryveagh Mtns

HEIGHT METRES	COUNTY	1:50K MAP NO.	MAP GRID REF	PROMINENCE	COUNTY RANK	MV RATING	DATE CLIMBED
751	Donegal	1	B928₂₆ 207₇₈	688m	9	7.9	

Lough Sallagh near Slieve Beagh SE Top, highpoint of County Monaghan

Corn Hill, highpoint of County Longford

CLASSIFICATION	MOUNTAIN NAME		ALTERNATIVE NAME				AREA
Ⓐ ⓋⓁ	**Benbaun**		Ir: Binn Bhán, 'white peak'				Twelve Bens

HEIGHT METRES	COUNTY	1:50K MAP NO.	MAP GRID REF	PROMINENCE	COUNTY RANK	MV RATING	DATE CLIMBED
729	Galway	37	L785$_{58}$ 539$_{03}$	684m	10	8.9	

CLASSIFICATION	MOUNTAIN NAME		ALTERNATIVE NAME				AREA
Ⓐ ⓋⓁ	**Knockboy**		Ir: An Cnoc Buí, 'yellow/golden hill'				Shehy/Knockboy

HEIGHT METRES	COUNTY	1:50K MAP NO.	MAP GRID REF	PROMINENCE	COUNTY RANK	MV RATING	DATE CLIMBED
706	Cork/ Kerry	85	W004$_{80}$ 620$_{60}$	685m	11	8.2	

CLASSIFICATION	MOUNTAIN NAME		ALTERNATIVE NAME				AREA
Ⓐ ⓋⓁ	**Sawel**		Ir: 'Samhail Phite Méabha,' 'resemblance of Maeve's vulva'				Sperrin Mtns

HEIGHT METRES	COUNTY	1:50K MAP NO.	MAP GRID REF	PROMINENCE	COUNTY RANK	MV RATING	DATE CLIMBED
678	Derry/Tyrone	13	H617$_{96}$ 973$_{05}$	657m	12	8.4	

CLASSIFICATION	MOUNTAIN NAME		ALTERNATIVE NAME				AREA
Ⓐ ⓋⓁ	**Cuilcagh**		Ir: Binn Chuilceach, 'chalky peak'				Cuilcagh Mtns

HEIGHT METRES	COUNTY	1:50K MAP NO.	MAP GRID REF	PROMINENCE	COUNTY RANK	MV RATING	DATE CLIMBED
665	Cavan/Fermanagh	26	H123$_{56}$ 280$_{17}$	570m	13	8.3	

CLASSIFICATION	MOUNTAIN NAME		ALTERNATIVE NAME				AREA
Ⓐ ⓋⓁ	**Truskmore**		Ir: Trosc Mór, 'big [obscure element]'				Dartry Mtns

HEIGHT METRES	COUNTY	1:50K MAP NO.	MAP GRID REF	PROMINENCE	COUNTY RANK	MV RATING	DATE CLIMBED
647	Sligo	16	G758$_{99}$ 473$_{48}$	560m	14	6.9	

CLASSIFICATION	MOUNTAIN NAME		ALTERNATIVE NAME				AREA
	Truskmore SE Cairn		Ir: Trosc Mór, 'big [obscure element]'				Dartry Mtns

HEIGHT METRES	COUNTY	1:50K MAP NO.	MAP GRID REF	PROMINENCE	COUNTY RANK	MV RATING	DATE CLIMBED
631	Leitrim	16	G763$_{14}$ 471$_{02}$	0m	15	6.5	

CLASSIFICATION	MOUNTAIN NAME		ALTERNATIVE NAME				AREA
Ⓐ	**Slieve Foye**		Ir: Sliabh Feá, 'mountain of rushes'				Cooley Mtns

HEIGHT METRES	COUNTY	1:50K MAP NO.	MAP GRID REF	PROMINENCE	COUNTY RANK	MV RATING	DATE CLIMBED
589	Louth	29/36A	J169$_{02}$ 119$_{34}$	494m	16	8.1	

CLASSIFICATION	MOUNTAIN NAME		ALTERNATIVE NAME				AREA
Ⓐ	**Slieve Gullion**		Ir: Sliabh gCuillinn, 'mtn of the steep slope/holly'				Slieve Gullion

HEIGHT METRES	COUNTY	1:50K MAP NO.	MAP GRID REF	PROMINENCE	COUNTY RANK	MV RATING	DATE CLIMBED
573	Armagh	29	J024$_{76}$ 203$_{31}$	478m	17	6.6	

CLASSIFICATION	MOUNTAIN NAME		ALTERNATIVE NAME				AREA
Ⓐ	**Trostan**		Ir: Trostán, 'pole/staff'				Antrim Hills

HEIGHT METRES	COUNTY	1:50K MAP NO.	MAP GRID REF	PROMINENCE	COUNTY RANK	MV RATING	DATE CLIMBED
550	Antrim	9	D179$_{61}$ 235$_{99}$	515m	18	6.6	

CLASSIFICATION	MOUNTAIN NAME	ALTERNATIVE NAME	AREA
Ⓐ	**Moylussa**		Slieve Bernagh

HEIGHT METRES	COUNTY	1:50K MAP NO.	MAP GRID REF	PROMINENCE	COUNTY RANK	MV RATING	DATE CLIMBED
531.6*	Clare	58	R648₄₄ 759₂₈	502m	19	6.2	

CLASSIFICATION	MOUNTAIN NAME	ALTERNATIVE NAME	AREA
Ⓐ	**Arderin**	Ir: Ard Éireann, 'the height of Ireland' or 'Eriu's height'	Slieve Blooms

HEIGHT METRES	COUNTY	1:50K MAP NO.	MAP GRID REF	PROMINENCE	COUNTY RANK	MV RATING	DATE CLIMBED
527	Laois/Offaly	54	S232₄₈ 989₀₄	420m	20	5.3	

CLASSIFICATION	MOUNTAIN NAME	ALTERNATIVE NAME	AREA
Ⓐ	**Brandon Hill**	Ir: Cnoc Bhréanail, 'hill of Bréanal'	Sth Midlands

HEIGHT METRES	COUNTY	1:50K MAP NO.	MAP GRID REF	PROMINENCE	COUNTY RANK	MV RATING	DATE CLIMBED
515	Kilkenny	68	S697₀₂ 402₆₇	450m	21	6.3	

CLASSIFICATION	MOUNTAIN NAME	ALTERNATIVE NAME	AREA
	Seltannasaggart SE Slope	Ir: Sailtean na Sagart, 'willow plantation of the priests'	Arigna Mtns

HEIGHT METRES	COUNTY	1:50K MAP NO.	MAP GRID REF	PROMINENCE	COUNTY RANK	MV RATING	DATE CLIMBED
412	Roscommon	26	G903₈₉ 195₅₁	0m	22	3.4	

CLASSIFICATION	MOUNTAIN NAME	ALTERNATIVE NAME	AREA
	Cupidstown Hill	Ir: Cnoc Bhaile Cupid, 'hill of Cupidstown'	Dublin/Wicklow

HEIGHT METRES	COUNTY	1:50K MAP NO.	MAP GRID REF	PROMINENCE	COUNTY RANK	MV RATING	DATE CLIMBED
379	Kildare	50	O005₇₃ 205₉₅	54m	23	3.0	

CLASSIFICATION	MOUNTAIN NAME	ALTERNATIVE NAME	AREA
	Slieve Beagh SE Top	Ir: Sliabh Beatha, prob. 'mountain of birch'	F'managh/S.Tyrone

HEIGHT METRES	COUNTY	1:50K MAP NO.	MAP GRID REF	PROMINENCE	COUNTY RANK	MV RATING	DATE CLIMBED
373	Monaghan	18	H531₈₅ 435₆₇	5m	24	6.6	

CLASSIFICATION	MOUNTAIN NAME	ALTERNATIVE NAME	AREA
	Corn Hill	Ir: Carn Clainne Aodha, 'cairn of Clann Aodha'	Nth Midlands

HEIGHT METRES	COUNTY	1:50K MAP NO.	MAP GRID REF	PROMINENCE	COUNTY RANK	MV RATING	DATE CLIMBED
278	Longford	34	N187₆₆ 842₁	203m	25	4.5	

CLASSIFICATION	MOUNTAIN NAME	ALTERNATIVE NAME	AREA
	Slieve Na Calliagh	Ir: Sliabh na Caillí, 'mountain of the hag'	Nth Midlands

HEIGHT METRES	COUNTY	1:50K MAP NO.	MAP GRID REF	PROMINENCE	COUNTY RANK	MV RATING	DATE CLIMBED
276	Meath	42	N586₁₇ 775₈₀	171m	26	6.0	

CLASSIFICATION	MOUNTAIN NAME	ALTERNATIVE NAME	AREA
	Mullaghmeen	Ir: Mullach Mín, 'smooth summit'	Nth Midlands

HEIGHT METRES	COUNTY	1:50K MAP NO.	MAP GRID REF	PROMINENCE	COUNTY RANK	MV RATING	DATE CLIMBED
258	Westmeath	41	N469₂₄ 793₇₉	146m	27	5.1	

The Mourne Wall rising to the summit of Slieve Donard, the highest mountain in Ulster

On the skyline the burial chamber at the summit of Slieve na Calliagh, highest hill of County Meath

107

THE HUNDRED HIGHEST IRISH MOUNTAINS

This list is the Hundred Highest with a prominence or drop from the summit of at least 100m.

	HEIGHT	MOUNTAIN NAME	1:50K MAP	MAP GRID REF	PROMINENCE	AREA/RANGE	DATE CLIMBED
1	1,038.6*	Carrauntoohil	78	V803₆₃ 844₂₁	1,038.6m	MacG'cuddy's Reeks	
2	988	Knocknapeasta	78	V835₈₇ 841₇₈	253m	MacG'cuddy's Reeks	
3	951.7*	Brandon	70	Q460₄₂ 1160₅	934m	Brandon Group	
4	925	Lugnaquillia	56	T032₁₇ 917₅₆	905m	Dublin/Wicklow	
5	917.9*	Galtymore	74	R878₄₆ 237₈₈	898m	Galty Mtns	
6	851	Baurtregaum	71	Q749₈₆ 076₆₇	643m	Slieve Mish	
7	850	Slieve Donard	29	J357₉₆ 276₉₀	822m	Mourne Mtns	
8	849	Mullaghcleevaun	56	006₇₆₃ 070₄₉	374m	Dublin/Wicklow	
9	840	Brandon Peak	70	Q472₀₇ 094₈₁	190m	Brandon Group	
10	839	Mangerton	78	V980₃₆ 807₈₅	584m	Mangerton	
11	835	Caherconree	71	Q733₁₈ 072₆₀	129m	Slieve Mish	
12	832	Purple Mtn	78	V886₄₀ 851₇₂	597m	Purple Mtns	
13	826	Beenoskee	70	Q580₆₂ 088₈₀	491m	Central Dingle	
14	825	Lyracappul	74	R845₆₂ 231₇₉	100m	Galty Mtns	
15	817	Tonelagee	56	008₅₀₃ 015₈₉	202m	Dublin/Wicklow	
16	814	Mweelrea	37	L789₈₃ 668₁₀	779m	Mweelrea Mtns	
17	806	Nephin	23/31	G103₄₇ 079₇₅	778m	North Mayo	
18	803	Ben Lugmore	37	L811₇₃ 673₇₉	158m	Mweelrea Mtns	
19	802	Greenane	74	R925₀₀ 239₂₇	157m	Galty Mtns	
20	795	Mount Leinster	68	S826₀₃ 526₀₈	707m	Blackstairs Mtns	
21	794	Knockmealdown	74	S057₉₇ 084₁₀	682m	K'mealdown Mtns	
22	792	Fauscoum	75	S316₈₉ 105₀₈	626m	Comeragh Mtns	
23	785	Temple Hill	74	R833₃₄ 218₃₀	190m	Galty Mtns	
24	784	Stumpa Dúloigh	78	V787₀₀ 793₈₄	499m	Dunkerron Mtns	
25	773	Mullaghanattin	78	V738₇₂ 772₇₆	528m	Dunkerron Mtns	
26	772	Barrclashcame	37	L849₅₁ 695₁₅	707m	Sheefry Hills	
27	772	Coomacarrea	78/83	V611₂₆ 825₃₅	457m	Glenbeigh H'shoe	
28	767	Slieve Commedagh	29	J346₁₀ 286₁₆	180m	Mourne Mtns	
29	764	Croagh Patrick	30	L905₈₅ 801₉₇	639m	Croagh Patrick	

indicates data updated or revised by MountainViews.ie

	HEIGHT	MOUNTAIN NAME	1:50K MAP	MAP GRID REF	PROMINENCE	AREA/RANGE	DATE CLIMBED
30	763	**Masatiompan**	70	Q465$_{32}$ 145$_{54}$	108m	Brandon Group	
31	758	**Camenabologue**	56	T023$_{21}$ 959$_{92}$	133m	Dublin/Wicklow	
32	757	**Kippure**	56	O115$_{82}$ 154$_{55}$	262m	Dublin/Wicklow	
33	755	**Knockanaffrin**	75	S285$_{60}$ 152$_{90}$	289m	Comeragh Mtns	
34	751	**Errigal**	1	B928$_{26}$ 207$_{78}$	688m	Donegal NW	
35	747	**Slieve Binnian**	29	J320$_{65}$ 233$_{55}$	283m	Mourne Mtns	
36	745	**Broaghnabinnia**	78	V801$_{63}$ 813$_{88}$	290m	Dunkerron Mtns	
37	745	**Slieve Bearnagh**	29	J313$_{16}$ 280$_{35}$	304m	Mourne Mtns	
38	735	**Blackstairs Mountain**	68	S810$_{59}$ 448$_{33}$	540m	Blackstairs Mtns	
39	734	**Conavalla**	56	T039$_{68}$ 971$_{58}$	109m	Dublin/Wicklow	
40	729	**Benbaun**	37	L785$_{58}$ 539$_{03}$	684m	Twelve Bens	
41	725	**Djouce**	56	O178$_{58}$ 103$_{60}$	200m	Dublin/Wicklow	
42	725	**Slieve Carr**	23	F914$_{93}$ 144$_{98}$	646m	North Mayo	
43	721	**Slievenamon**	67	S297$_{82}$ 307$_{22}$	711m	South Midlands	
44	718	**Gravale**	56	O104$_{90}$ 094$_{20}$	123m	Dublin/Wicklow	
45	716	**Corranabinnia**	30	F903$_{07}$ 031$_{65}$	541m	North Mayo	
46	715	**Meenteog**	78/83	V638$_{01}$ 826$_{61}$	110m	Glenbeigh H'shoe	
47	711	**Bencorr**	37	L811$_{66}$ 522$_{00}$	306m	Twelve Bens	
48	708	**Slieve Meelbeg**	29	J300$_{75}$ 279$_{18}$	193m	Mourne Mtns	
49	706	**Knockboy**	85	W004$_{80}$ 620$_{60}$	685m	Shehy/Knockboy	
50	704	**Slievelamagan**	29	J328$_{97}$ 260$_{52}$	199m	Mourne Mtns	
51	703	**Moanbane**	56	O033$_{33}$ 068$_{86}$	108m	Dublin/Wicklow	
52	702	**Binn idir an dá Log**	37	L888$_{20}$ 528$_{27}$	644m	Maamturks	
53	700	**Ben Gorm**	37	L861$_{84}$ 652$_{33}$	670m	Ben Gorm Mtns	
54	698	**Birreencorragh**	23/31	G024$_{56}$ 050$_{07}$	583m	North Mayo	
55	696	**Bencollaghduff**	37	L797$_{80}$ 529$_{93}$	191m	Twelve Bens	
56	694	**Keeper Hill**	59	R823$_{97}$ 666$_{97}$	627m	Shannon	
57	694	**The Paps East**	79	W133$_{22}$ 855$_{43}$	623m	Paps/D'nasaggart	
58	692	**Caoinkeen**	85	W010$_{40}$ 645$_{57}$	107m	Shehy/Knockboy	
59	691	**Benbreen**	37	L783$_{11}$ 515$_{47}$	186m	Twelve Bens	

HEIGHT	MOUNTAIN NAME	1:50K MAP	MAP GRID REF	PROMINENCE	AREA/RANGE	DATE CLIMBED
60 690	Knocknadobar	83	V506₄₈ 845₁₆	565m	Iveragh NW	
61 690	The Paps West	79	W125₀₃ 855₂₈	106m	Paps/D'nasaggart	
62 688	Croaghaun	22/30	F559₆₂ 060₉₁	688m	Achill/Corraun	
63 685	Hungry Hill	84	V760₈₈ 497₂₆	400m	Caha Mtns	
64 684	Knockmoyle	78/83	V665₁₄ 749₈₂	169m	Dunkerron Mtns	
65 682	Maumtrasna	38	L960₈₉ 637₄₂	607m	Partry/Joyce C'try	
66 681	Caherbarnagh	79	W191₆₁ 871₇₅	361m	Paps/D'nasaggart	
67 680	Slieve Meelmore	29	J305₉₄ 287₀₂	109m	Mourne Mtns	
68 679	Colly	78/83	V650₇₃ 807₆₁	144m	Glenbeigh H'shoe	
69 678	Sawel	13	H617₉₆ 973₀₅	657m	Sperrin Mtns	
70 678	Slieve Snacht	1	B923₅₉ 148₁₂	403m	Donegal NW	
71 677	Derryclare	37	L815₀₉ 510₄₈	129m	Twelve Bens	
72 676	Knocknagantee	78/83	V667₉₈ 729₉₄	101m	Dunkerron Mtns	
73 674.7*	An Bheann Mhór	83	V593₅₈ 683₄₈	290m	Dunkerron Mtns	
74 674	Croaghgorm	11	G948₃₂ 895₈₅	541m	Bluestack Mtns	
75 674	Slieve Muck	29	J281₁₂ 249₉₉	159m	Mourne Mtns	
76 671	Lavagh More	11	G932₃₁ 910₁₀	193m	Bluestack Mtns	
77 671	Slievemore	22/30	F650₃₇ 086₆₉	582m	Achill/Corraun	
78 670	Slievanea NE Top	70	Q515₈₀ 063₆₁	265m	Central Dingle	
79 668	Knocknafallia	74	S090₀₉ 076₁₂	153m	K'mealdown Mtns	
80 667	Finnararagh	78	V696₇₃ 737₃₁	142m	Dunkerron Mtns	
81 667	Letterbreckaun	37	L856₅₅ 550₉₇	322m	Maamturks	
82 667.1*	Muckish	2	C004₄₈ 287₀₈	522m	Donegal NW	
83 666	Coomura Mtn	78/83	V677₂₃ 751₇₈	111m	Dunkerron Mtns	
84 665	Cuilcagh	26	H123₅₆ 280₁₇	570m	Breifne	
85 664	Bengower	37	L783₀₁ 506₄₄	196m	Twelve Bens	
86 664	Croaghanmoira	62	T099₂₂ 865₀₄	209m	Dublin/Wicklow	
87 663	Sugarloaf Hill	74	S039₇₀ 104₇₉	118m	K'mealdown Mtns	
88 661	Binn Mhór	44	L918₄₁ 493₅₅	406m	Maamturks	
89 660	Beenmore	83	V596₄₀ 867₉₁	125m	Glenbeigh H'shoe	
90 658	Knockowen	84	V808₇₀ 553₉₃	373m	Caha Mtns	

A bleak and lonely plateau: Maumtrasna's remote summit cairn

Coomeeneragh Lake near Meenteog on the Glenbeigh Horseshoe, County Kerry

91	657	**Mullacor**	56	T092$_{71}$ 939$_{13}$	102m	Dublin/Wicklow
92	656	**Chimney Rock Mtn**	29	J364$_{09}$ 257$_{21}$	131m	Mourne Mtns
93	655	**Cove Mtn**	29	J336$_{66}$ 270$_{84}$	100m	Mourne Mtns
94	654	**Muckanaght**	37	L767$_{83}$ 540$_{83}$	179m	Twelve Bens
95	654	**Keadeen Mtn**	62	S953$_{95}$ 897$_{64}$	334m	Dublin/Wicklow
96	652	**Dooish**	6	B982$_{21}$ 210$_{37}$	377m	Donegal NW
97	652	**Knockshanahullion**	74	R999$_{56}$ 104$_{43}$	317m	K'mealdown Mtns
98	650	**Crohane**	79	W049$_{71}$ 829$_{67}$	385m	Mangerton
99	650	**Mullaghanish**	79	W214$_{32}$ 817$_{83}$	264m	Paps/D'nasaggart
100	648.9*	**Coomcallee**	83/84	V623$_{92}$ 677$_{20}$	105m	Dunkerron Mtns

MOUNTAINVIEWS AREA LISTINGS

AREA NAME	NO. SUMMITS	MAX HEIGHT	AVG HEIGHT	AVG RATING	AVG CLIMBED
Achill/Corraun	11	688m	579m	85	96.8
Antrim Hills	20	550m	438m	63	50.8
Arigna Mountains	3	458m	428m	41	28.6
Ballyhoura Mountains	8	528m	475m	61	47.0
Belfast Hills	3	478m	364m	52	43.6
Ben Gorm Mountains	3	700m	694m	88	113.3
Blackstairs Mountains	11	795m	607m	76	113.9
Bluestack Mountains	35	674m	553m	83	34.1
Boggeragh Mountains	9	644m	492m	48	24.8
Brandon Group	13	952m	831m	86	323.3
Breifne	12	665m	574m	75	80.4
Bricklieve/Curlew	3	359m	322m	61	19.4
Caha Mountains	39	685m	547m	83	44.9
Central Dingle	19	826m	584m	83	42.8
Comeragh Mountains	17	792m	672m	74	133.8
Cooley/Gullion	13	589m	490m	69	174.0
Croagh Patrick	5	764m	726m	70	668.3
Dartry Mountains	28	647m	512m	77	77.4
Dingle West	11	516m	332m	74	42.3
Donegal NW	54	751m	537m	79	153.1
Donegal SW	16	595m	528m	77	109.8
Dublin/Wicklow	89	925m	624m	62	369.6
Dunkerron Mountains	46	784m	617m	83	40.4
East Coast	2	251m	220m	43	75.3
Fermanagh/Sth Tyrone	6	398m	367m	60	27.9
Galty Mountains	23	919m	759m	74	329.9
Glenbeigh Horseshoe	17	772m	616m	83	46.1
Inishowen	22	615m	389m	73	28.3
Iveragh NW	16	690m	388m	72	25.1

AREA NAME	NO. SUMMITS	MAX HEIGHT	AVG HEIGHT	AVG RATING	AVG CLIMBED
Keenaght	3	399m	391m	70	26.3
Knockmealdown Mtns	14	794m	657m	69	189.6
Maamturks	19	702m	611m	87	133.8
MacGillycuddy's Reeks	28	1039m	931m	86	618.9
Mangerton	22	839m	653m	75	178.1
Mizen/Sheeps Head	9	407m	297m	67	13.1
Mourne Mountains	47	850m	631m	76	305.7
Mweelrea Mountains	8	814m	766m	91	327.2
Nagles Mountains	4	428m	417m	54	16.7
North Kerry	2	267m	247m	48	7.8
North Mayo	38	806m	573m	83	54.2
North Midlands	10	339m	267m	53	52.3
North Wexford	4	420m	323m	48	19.0
Ox Mountains	4	544m	372m	62	30.2
Paps/Derrynasaggart	18	694m	592m	67	69.5
Partry/Joyce Country	16	682m	549m	82	39.6
Purple Mountain	4	832m	784m	86	235.1
S. Donegal/W. Tyrone	7	451m	343m	56	8.5
Shannon	43	694m	471m	56	40.4

Beenbo (left) faces Beenatoor (right), framing a view of the sea north of the Dingle Peninsula

Sheefry Hills	7	772m	651m	82	55.2
Shehy/Knockboy	43	706m	538m	69	26.5
Slieve Bloom	10	527m	485m	49	64.9
Slieve Mish	14	851m	678m	82	67.6
Slieve Miskish	5	490m	337m	69	9.9
South Connemara	6	358m	325m	69	16.3
South Midlands	11	721m	471m	60	86.6
South Wexford	3	270m	250m	51	19.8
Sperrin Mountains	51	678m	493m	70	44.3
Twelve Bens	30	729m	612m	84	134.0
W. Limerick/N. Kerry	9	451m	389m	45	10.0
West Clare	4	391m	320m	69	36.2

On the website slight changes occur as a result of user interaction. Also on the website, it is possible to sort by any of the categories, such as 'Average Rating'. If you do this you can more easily see that, say, the highest-rated areas are Mweelrea Mountains followed by Ben Gorm Mountains and Maamturks while the least is the open-cast mined Arigna Mountains.

Similarly the most climbed on average are Dublin/Wicklow followed by MacGillycuddy's Reeks and Purple Mountain while the least is the North Kerry group, having only about 3% of the recorded climbs of the most climbed.

The scarred and industrial summit of Seltannasaggart in the Arigna Mountains

APPENDIX: ORIGINS AND DISCUSSION OF LISTS

Previous lists

What we mean by 'previous lists' are those that are immediate ancestors to the MountainViews lists. There are a number of other valuable lists of Irish summits such as those compiled by William Docharty, Dave Hewitt, Clem Clements and Claude Wall. This is a topic for another document.

For introductory references, look at ***www.ldwa.org.uk/hillwalkers/ register4.php*** and ***www.hills-database.co.uk/index.html***

Joss Lynam

In 1952, Joss Lynam, with help from C. R. P. Vandeleur, created a list of 2,000-footers. In a private email of 3 December 2009 Joss mentioned some of the circumstances regarding the list. An early difficulty was the quality of maps that existed at the time (see correspondence with Joss Lynam, p. 120). He also mentioned in an email to Simon Stewart that all four copies of the original 1952 list appeared to be mislaid.

The Federation of Mountaineering Clubs of Ireland (FMCI) reprint in 1976 of Claude Wall's *Mountaineering in Ireland* (1939) included the '2000ft list', listing some 257 summits in total.

In 1997 Joss Lynam produced a version of the '600m List' dated 20 September 1997. In April 1999 Joss produced a revised version of the '600m List', including some 278 summits, an extensive introduction and some summarised statistics.

In 1999 the Mountaineering Council of Ireland (MCI) website, then with Simon Stewart as editor, published data from the Joss Lynam 1999 list and popularised an automated tool for producing lists to arbitrary specifications. (A modern version is currently at http://mountainviews.ie/ mv/irl150setup.htm.)

In 2001 Joss created a document amending his 1999 list with some 39 corrections ('600m List-Revised June99.doc'). There is no date on this document; however, it was emailed on 30 July 2001.

In 2001 the MCI website listing was altered to incorporate the aforementioned corrections. (Unfortunately, the revised MCI website of 2005 did not include any listing of summits or the link to the automated tool for producing lists.)

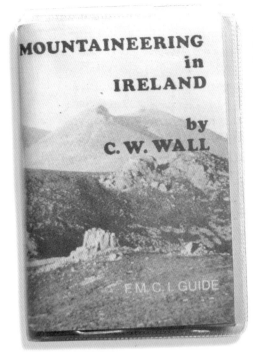

The 1976 FMCI reprint of Claude Wall's *Mountaineering in Ireland*, which included the '2,000ft list'.

MountainViews first encountered the Myrddyn Phillips/Michael Dewey list as a handwritten document with accompanying letter dated 23 November 2002, with modifications dated 15 January 2003. Both of these were forwarded by Joss Lynam to Simon Stewart with a note saying 'Simon, over to you, Joss.' MountainViews understand that this list was heavily influenced by Clem Clements, a respected UK summit list creator.

From a private email from Myrddyn Phillips, we understand that in 1998 Michael Dewey produced a listing of the 500m tops of Ireland. In 2000 Myrddyn privately produced a listing to the 500m tops of Ireland. To quote: 'The criteria and format of the list was based upon Michael's 500-Metre Tops of England and Wales listing that had been published by Constable in I think 1995. Copies of the Irish list were sent to various people including Michael Dewey and Mountaineering Ireland.'

Following this Myrddyn Phillips started cooperating with Michael Dewey and in November 2000 jointly produced 'the 500m Tops of Ireland'. This joint listing was published on Michael's website. Myrddyn Phillips then sent a copy to the Mountaineering Council of Ireland.

MountainViews Revisions

While we will always acknowledge the origins of the list, after thousands of amendments and measurements in the field, etc, the lists can now fairly be said to be the collective work of MountainViews and its members.

2002:

— MountainViews published a combined 500m and 600m list as described in the 'Previous Lists' section above, in June.

— Consultation about this list proceeded before the list was made public by email with interested parties, such as Joss Lynam who submitted corrections in document '600mForJossCorrectedByJoss.xls' on 16 March 2002. A list of other people who have assisted with list development is recorded on http://mountainviews.ie/credits/

2003: MountainViews published a revised version in September 2003 with fairly minor amendments.

2005: MountainViews published a revised version with some corrections.

2006: Revised 500m and 600m lists with geographical corrections and extensive summit naming from P. D. Tempan. Area names codified following initial consultation.

2007: Added 380 400m summits, all geographically checked by MountainViews members with substantial name research.

2008: Added 208 150m prominence summits under 400m, all geographically checked by MountainViews members with substantial name research. Prominence data added for summits below 500m. Area names expanded to handle the often dispersed smaller summits. Mountain sub-area names added.

2009: Further additions to name information and complete geographical check on summits over 500m including completion of prominence data with 'linking col' and 'nearest higher' fields. Refinements made to area and sub-area names.

Summit lists were codified, such as the Arderins, introduced

Looking southwest from the summit of Corraun to Achillbeg Island, and the distant Clare Island

in June 2009 to describe 500m summits. The term 'Vandeleur-Lynam' started to be formally used by MountainViews to describe those of the 600m summits which conform to the Vandeleur-Lynam specification. The specific term 'Vandeleur-Lynam' was not in general use as a list name prior to MountainViews using the term. Joss Lynam himself had called it the '600m List'.

Others, such as Peter Wilson (ref: www.ucd.ie/gsi/pdf/34-1/hills. pdf), had referred as follows: LYNAM, J. (1997) 600 metre mountain top list for Ireland. Dublin: Mountaineering Council of Ireland.

When mentioned to Joss Lynam, he consented to the use of the term 'Vandeleur-Lynam' by MountainViews.ie, agreed its specification and even came up with an abbreviation ('Vanlyn').

2010: Further changes were made including using work from Jim Bloomer (now committee member of the UK-based Database of British and Irish Hills, or DoBIH). These changes were not published, however, until 2011. Corrections made to the County Highpoints list.

2011: Outstanding changes made and 2010 version published. Some new sub-area names created.

2012: Work continued on the extension of the lists to 100m prominence, correcting list membership by precision surveying and making the usual corrections from members.

Separate Tops and Modern Prominence-based Lists

Joss Lynam included the distinction between 'separate' and 'subsidiary' tops; however, he had considerable misgivings about this. In the introductory notes to the 2,000ft list in *Mountaineering in Ireland* (1976) he said: 'The difference between separate mountains and subsidiary tops is ill-defined, and the decision is a personal one which cannot be insisted upon.' In the introduction to the '600m List' (1999), he stated:

> Entries have been divided into separate mountains and subsidiary tops ... I was in two minds as to whether to retain the distinction. It was pointed out to me that walkers who had completed the list did not distinguish between the two classes, that the distinction was essentially subjective, and that the only other List to retain them was Munros. I finally decided in favour for compatability with the original List and for the purely practical reason that I would have to start dreaming up names for all those 'North Tops' etc.

Most modern lists, such as those of MountainViews.ie, have striven to remove such subjective criteria. How can someone say they have ascended all the 'separate tops' of a list if that subset is liable to change based on someone else's subjective definition? Modern lists are now characterised by height and prominence, so a list will state something like '500m with a prominence of 30m'. (The Irish Arderins follow that standard. The British Marilyns follow the convention of a minimum prominence of 150m which implies a minimum height of 150m.)

A further advantage of establishing the height and prominence of summits is that the creation of shorter lists is facilitated. For example, if you require a shorter list of summits, simply apply a greater prominence requirement. (MountainViews does this in its Hundred Highest of 100m prominence list.)

Although the modern criteria are more definite and flexible in use, they are not without difficulties of their own. How do you establish what exact height and prominence a summit has? As Joss's comment about the 1952 list shows, it was difficult to create lists based on geographical information because of inadequate data. However, the situation is improving year by year. The OSi 1:50,000 maps have 10m contours and often have spot-heights which are considerably more accurate than the 1-inch maps.

Hillwalkers' hill-surveying techniques have been codified, for example, by the publishers of the DoBIH. Modern surveying GPS units operating with base station differential correction in Ireland now offer 0.1m accuracy, which is sufficient to resolve most borderline cases, and MountainViews volunteers have been doing this. (Note: this is not the same as consumer GPS units which currently offer vertical accuracy of only a few metres, useful only for indication rather than exact measurement.) Nevertheless, it will be some years before the summits whose height or prominence is on the borderline between different categories can finally be established. MountainViews has a programme to achieve this.

Some Correspondence with Joss Lynam Regarding Lists
This section includes some points made made by Joss Lynam to Simon Stewart regarding his ideas on mountain lists for Ireland. We include them for background interest and because Joss was a major authority in Irish hillwalking and his views will continue to be important for many years.

Email from Joss Lynam, 7 June 2009:

Thanks for Mountain Views [newsletter]. Name for 500m – I like Arderin [as a name for a list]. I always heard that at one time it was thought to be the highest mtn in Ireland.

Name for 600m. When it was first made out as a 2000ft List it was agreed to call it them 'Vandeleurs' after the man who had walked most of them. Just as a Munro has stayed a Munro I've presumed that a 600m would still be a Vandeleur.

Arising out of that, and your suggestion of a symbol for significant summits. Significant? Difficult to define – there'd be endless discussion. Better surely to use height like the BMC Scottish maps. To use 600m provides a round of nearly 300 summits, like the Munros, in number if not in difficulty.

There was some discussion about whether the V-L list should continue with a prominence of 15m or 30m. Both approaches have advantages and disadvantages. Simon Stewart met with Joss at his house on 6 November 2009 and discussed the future of the list. The main conclusions were:

▲ Reaffirmation that the V-L list should be based on height and prominence. The list should be changed if there is strong evidence that a given summit does or does not meet a specific height or prominence standard.

▲ Reaffirmation that the standard for the V-L list is 600m height, 15m prominence. While there might have been some advantages in bringing the prominence of the V-L list into line with other lists at 30m or other approaches such as the '1-2-5' principle of some metric lists, it was agreed that the V-L list would continue with the 15m prominence.

Email from Joss Lynam, 3 December 2009:

Thanks for Mountain View [newsletter] and the remarks about the LV List. Could I put in a short para? The List was actually issued in 1952, based on the half-inch (1:126,720) scale map which is all we had, except the one inch scale maps for Wicklow and Kerry. The V.I. on both was 100ft, except on the 1", it was 250ft above 1000ft. People will understand how a height difference of 25ft might slip in. The revised edition of Claude Wall's Mountaineering in Ireland was published in 1975. [Simon Stewart assisted Joss Lynam with the printing of various books, including this revision, while working in the printing trade in the 1970s.]

Email from Joss Lynam, 2 January 2010 (in reference to position markers on revised OSi maps which use MV data and mention the V-L list):

Mountaintop spots – happy that 600+ etc should be marked, but I'd expected a small triangle or other shape, but I'm not going to get excited about it. [In fact OSi chose the round shape of the markers from a selection presented by 'madfrankie', a graphic designer member of MountainViews.]

Publication of the MountainViews Lists
The summit lists continue to be published in new places which so far include:

▲ The MountainViews.ie website where it is presented as individual summits with comments and photos or as lists where summits can be logged. Coverage with comments is 100 per cent for the Vandeleur-Lynam and Arderin lists.

▲ MountainViews also publishes the list in a form useable as waypoints or POI (points of interest) on a GPS, using the member corrected summit horizontal positions. Coverage for this in early 2012) was around 97 per cent for the Vandeleur-Lynam list and 74 per cent for the current overall list of 1,057 summits.

▲ MountainViews data is used by OpenStreetMap

▲ MountainViews data was used by the OSi (Ordnance Survey Ireland) Trailmaster project

▲ Walking World Ireland presented a listing of the Arderins in 2009

▲ MountainViews data used to create summit classification and position markers on the currently reprinting OSi 1:50,000 *Discovery* map series.

▲ The UK-based Database of British and Irish Hills uses some of the naming and classification data from MountainViews. In general, agreement with their lists is good, which validates both as geographical information was usually arrived at independently.

FURTHER READING

A personal introduction to summiteering

Written by Mark Brennan, this describes the several very human stages by which he got involved with MountainViews starting as an occasional user and ending as a committee member.

Url: *MountainViews.ie/book/VLAGuide2013/SummiteeringIntro.pdf*

An introduction to Irish hill surveying

Written by John FitzGerald, this article describes how MountainViews is going about establishing the geographical information for the lists that we promote.

Url: *MountainViews.ie/book/VLAGuide2013/IrishHillSurveying.pdf*

Corrections & errata

Where there are changes in geographical information about summits listed, for example in position or height of a summit or its membership of a relevant list then this will be reflected in the pages of the website. Should there be changes in the articles in the book then these will be placed online at: *MountainViews.ie/book/VLAGuide2013/Amendments.pdf*